VIRTUAL INEQUALITY

American Governance and Public Policy series
Series Editor: Barry Rabe, University of Michigan

VIRTUAL INEQUALITY
Beyond the Digital Divide

KAREN MOSSBERGER

CAROLINE J. TOLBERT

MARY STANSBURY

Georgetown University Press
Washington, D.C.

Georgetown University Press, Washington, D.C.
© 2003 by Georgetown University Press. All rights reserved.
Printed in the United States of America

10 9 8 7 6 5 4 3 2 1   2003

This book is printed on acid-free recycled paper meeting the requirements
of the American National Standard for Permanence in Paper for Printed
Library Materials.

Library of Congress Cataloging-in-Publication Data

Mossberger, Karen.
Virtual inequality : beyond the digital divide / Karen Mossberger, Caroline J.
Tolbert, Mary Stansbury.
    p. cm. – (American governance and public policy series)
Includes bibliographical reference and index.
    ISBN 0-87840-999-8 (pbk. : alk. paper)
1. Digital divide. I. Tolbert, Caroline J. II. Stansbury, Mary
Catherine, 1957– III. Title. IV. American governance and public policy.
    HN49 .I56M67 2003
    303 .48'33—dc21
                                                    2003004571

Contents

List of Tables and Figure

Tables

Figure

Preface

The issue of the "digital divide"—or disparities in information technology based on demographic factors such as race, ethnicity, income, education, and gender—captured headlines as the Internet made otherwise steady progress in permeating American society. Casting a shadow over the country's newfound fascination with the information "superhighway" were persistent reports that the poor, minorities, and others remained disconnected. The numbers contained in the reports were troubling indicators of a potential problem, but they said little about the causes or consequences of the problem and the possible remedies. For example, was the problem affordability or the ability to learn how to use the technology? Was it the ability to find and use the information on the Internet? Was it a lack of awareness of the possible uses and benefits of information technology? And what difference did it make anyway, even if some people never use computers and the Internet—would they and society be appreciably worse off? Much of the prior research has focused less on these questions than on counting the number of people who have access to technology at home. This is a first step—as Deborah Stone has said, counting is a political act and raises awareness of an issue—but it does little to inform debate or to offer guidance to policymakers.[1]

To us, there was a larger story to be told, and through telling the story we could better define the problem and appropriately target public resources. The real story of the "digital divide" could be found by understanding more about the experiences, attitudes, and needs of the individuals caught in the gap. A survey that focused on low-income communities and included a number of minority individuals would enable those most affected to tell their own story. By thinking about why disparities in information technology are a policy issue—about the possible consequences for society and for normative values such as equality of opportunity—we could also begin to move "beyond the digital divide" as an issue of access and to provoke a fuller public discussion about what the aims and obligations of public policy should be.

Our interdisciplinary team of three Kent State University researchers brought different perspectives to the topic. Mary Stansbury is a professor of library and information science, and her previous research on underserved populations sensitized her to this issue early on, particularly because public libraries became a focal point for public access to technology. Mary sought out faculty from the university's graduate program in public policy to carry out collaborative research on the issue and found two political scientists eager to take up the challenge—Caroline Tolbert, who had conducted research on issues such as race and ethnicity and direct democracy, and Karen Mossberger, who specialized in urban policy. Together we obtained research support from a national foundation and the Ohio Board of Regents, in order to conduct a national, random-sample telephone survey that included a separate sample drawn from low-income communities.

The results of that survey form the basis of this book, but we hope that what we present is much more than an aggregation of data. Our aim is to push the boundaries of the policy debate and make the information accessible to a wide audience.

We hope to influence the debate on this issue by redefining it as multidimensional—through consideration of an access divide, a skills divide, an economic opportunity divide, and a democratic divide. Although Pippa Norris's excellent cross-national study, in which she uses the term the "democratic divide," differs in many ways from ours, we share her concern that the relationship between technology disparities and public objectives merit more discussion.[2] We argue that public policy needs to address issues of skill as well as access and be focused on the way in which access and skill influence economic opportunity and political participation, now and in the future.

Our research is presented in a way that requires no knowledge of statistical methods, even though the study has been conducted according to academic standards and uses more sophisticated analysis than most of the prior studies on technology access. We hope to reach policymakers, interested citizens, and all sorts of thoughtful individuals who are engaged in this issue but who may not have formal training in statistics and research methods. Throughout the text, we use "What Matters" boxes to highlight the results that are statistically significant and to keep track of what might be an otherwise confusing array of outcomes on a number of questions. We list "what matters" without the numbers or with simple probabilities. Behind these simple comparisons, however, are multivariate regression analyses that statistically control for the effect of multiple influences, and we offer the regression tables in the appendix for those who are interested in examining our statistical findings in more detail. We discuss our methods to some extent within the text, because we feel that this is an important advantage of the research presented here. In the interest of reaching as broad an audience as possible, though, we carefully explain our approach in clear language and leave the more detailed and technical discussions for the endnotes. In short, we hope to change the landscape of policy debate by moving beyond the limitations of current research and beyond the definition of the problem as one primarily based on access.

Notes

1. Stone 2002, 176.
2. Norris 2001.

Acknowledgments

A project such as this one—a book based on a national survey—
is inevitably the product of many people, not just the authors.
We are indebted to our sponsors at a national foundation
(which makes it a policy to withhold publicity for all grants). The
challenge grant we received from the Ohio Board of Regents provided
crucial funding, allowing us to proceed without delay. The Computer-Assisted Telephone Interviewing Laboratory in Kent State's
Department of Sociology provided trained interviewers, supervision,
and consultation for the survey. Tom Hensley, chair of the political
science department, supported this project in many ways beyond the
call of duty. We also thank Rick Rubin, interim dean for the College
of Communications, Joseph Danks, dean of the College of Arts and
Sciences, and Richard Worthington, dean of the College of Fine and
Professional Arts.

We have noted on several chapters special assistance from two of
our graduate research assistants—Ramona McNeal and Lisa Dotterweich, who are doctoral students in the public policy program in Kent
State University's Department of Political Science. Carrie Hribar, also
a public policy graduate student, and Tinnie Banks, of the College of
Education, provided valuable research assistance as well.

A number of colleagues and other observers offered comments on
initial data, arguments, or early chapters presented at conferences
such as the American Library Association, American Political Science
Association, Midwest Political Science Association, Western Political
Science Association, American Society for Information Science and
Technology, and Association of Internet Researchers. Among those
we thank for their insights are Larry Ledebur, Genie Stowers, Paul
Baker, Rodney Hero, Hal Wolman, Susan Clarke, Donald Norris,
and two anonymous reviewers. We tried to follow your suggestions,
and we hope that it shows. Barry Rabe and Gail Grella, of Georgetown University Press, gave us sage advice throughout this process,

and we are grateful to be working with a publishing team of Georgetown's caliber.

We appreciate the efforts of the more than 1,800 people who answered our survey questions, in an age when telemarketers and others mercilessly clog the telephone lines. We thank the government officials and community activists in Berkeley, California, who took time to welcome us to the city and answer our questions.

Finally, we thank those who are closest to us for their support over the past two years, especially our spouses and our children (who range from ages one to twenty-two). One theme that emerges from this book is the role that young people will play in developing the social potential of information technology. In that spirit, we dedicate this book to our children: Heather, Lauren, Jacqueline, Eveline, Edward, Amanda, Elizabeth, and Thomas.

Chapter 1

Redefining the Digital Divide

Information technology is now an integral part of the workplace and the home for many Americans. More than half of American households now use the Internet, and two-thirds own home computers. Their presence transforms the way in which we work, play, socialize, and discover and disseminate information.

While the use of information technology is growing rapidly, some segments of society remain largely disconnected from this trend. The term "digital divide" has been used to describe the patterns of unequal access to information technology based on income, race, ethnicity, gender, age, and geography that surfaced during the mid-1990s. Data showing that computer ownership and Internet access are lower among certain groups of the population have generated both a spate of public and private initiatives and a chorus of critics who dismiss the divide as either a myth or of little real consequence. Heated controversy currently surrounds federal programs addressing the digital divide, as congressional proponents of these efforts battle attempts by the Bush administration to eliminate them.

We aim to contribute to these debates and to public policy in this area by providing a more accurate assessment of the problem and more information about the needs, attitudes, and experiences of the low-income and minority communities that have been the focus of current initiatives. The research presented here is distinctive in two ways.

First, we advocate moving beyond the narrow boundaries of the way in which the digital divide is currently defined. The preponderance of programs, debate, and research has been restricted to the problem of *access* to technology. But having access to a computer is insufficient if individuals lack the skills they need to take advantage of technology. Skills development has taken a backseat to the provision of wiring and hardware in most programs, and there is scant research evidence on skills. Moreover, little is known about the experiences or attitudes of disadvantaged groups in relation to the public objectives that support government intervention—economic opportunity and political participation. We propose a broader definition of the problem as consisting of multiple divides: an access divide, a skills divide, an economic opportunity divide, and a democratic divide.[1]

Second, our research has several advantages over existing studies because of its breadth, its low-income sample, and its methods of analysis. As suggested by the multiple divides, the survey on which this book is based includes a wide-ranging set of policy concerns beyond access. In order to paint an accurate picture of the attitudes and experiences of disadvantaged groups, we surveyed a random sample of respondents from high-poverty census tracts, as well as a more general sample for comparison. Finally, nearly all of the existing data have been reported as simple percentages. These percentages are useful for understanding general trends, but they cannot sort out the relative significance of different factors in the same way that statistical methods such as multivariate regression can. Using these methods, we can distinguish the causes of technology disparities, or the differences that matter. Nevertheless, we present the results of our study in a way that requires no statistical background, as explained later in this chapter. Together, our research and analysis allow us to explore new ground in the multiple divides and to test the validity of previous conclusions about access and other issues that were not based on multivariate statistics.

In this chapter, we trace the evolution of the "digital divide" as a policy issue, explain our approach and research methods, and offer an overview of the chapters that follow, particularly the different objectives that we set out to achieve in each.

Issue Evolution: The Access Divide and Beyond

Once the province of scientists, the Internet's potential as mass medium was unleashed by the development of a graphically based web browser in 1994, which made use of the web possible through a few simple clicks of a mouse. In 1995, Vice President Al Gore announced the development of a National Information Infrastructure—the information superhighway—as a priority of the Clinton administration. Also during 1995, the first of several studies undertaken by the National Telecommunications and Information Administration (NTIA) appeared. The report, *Falling through the Net: A Survey of the "Have Nots" in Rural and Urban America,* revealed inequities in access to personal computers and the Internet.[2] Subsequently, the Telecommunications Act of 1996 extended telecommunications policy beyond traditional concerns with phone service to include new digital media. This represented the first policy response to the disparities featured in the NTIA report and also established this issue as a problem of access, akin to telephone service, which has been cross-subsidized in rural regions by national taxes on telephone utilities. As part of this act, the E-Rate program, funded by taxes on local and long distance telephone carriers, provides schools and libraries in poor communities with discounted rates for Internet access, high-speed data connections, phone service, and wiring.[3]

Later iterations of the NTIA study have tracked changes in computer and Internet access over the ensuing years. The exact origin of the term "digital divide" is unclear, but it became popular after NTIA used the phrase to describe disparities in access in its 1998 report.[4] As discussed in the next chapter, home access has continued to be a central concern in research, although later studies also examined access in various places.[5]

Access concerns predominate in programs as well as research addressing the technologically disadvantaged. The E-Rate is the largest federal program, with total spending of about $2.25 billion in fiscal year (FY) 2001 for technology infrastructure. Two other federal programs, the Technologies Opportunities Program (TOP) and the Community Technology Centers (CTC) assist communities with other needs, such as hardware, software, content development, and training. Federal resources committed to skills development are decidedly more modest than infrastructure investment. The TOP supports pilot projects, and the CTC program funds about 400 centers nationwide. Together, their spending totaled only $110 million in FY 2001, or about 5 percent of the amount expended on E-Rate.

Federal efforts are supplemented by private initiatives. That the issue of the digital divide has captured the imagination of many is evident in the programs funded by foundations, corporations, and non-profits. The Digital Divide Network lists approximately 20,000 initiatives in its directory, but many of these programs are small-scale, with a few notable exceptions, such as the Gates Foundation's assistance for public libraries.[6]

Federal policy still constitutes a mainstay of funding in this policy area and is now the focus of controversy over future policy direction. Existing policy supports public access in schools, libraries, and community centers, but proposals to partially subsidize the purchase of computers or Internet services for low-income families have also circulated in Washington in the past.[7] To date, however, home access has been supported primarily through small nonprofit programs that offer loans and used computers to low-income families.

More recently, conflict has erupted on Capitol Hill over the fate of the CTC and TOP programs, which the Bush administration designated for termination. Clashes over federal policy revolve around two issues: whether disparities will disappear of their own accord, in light of the rapid diffusion of the Internet, and whether government intervention is appropriate, regardless of continued inequities. The 2002 installment of the NTIA reports takes a decidedly optimistic turn, entitling its findings "A Nation Online," in contrast to the "digital divide" of a few years ago.[8] Contained within the report, however, are data that show that rapid diffusion has not yet erased previous disparities. Will this gap eventually close through the natural course of events, without the commitment of public revenues? If not, is promoting digital equity even a legitimate policy goal?

In the chapters that follow, we offer evidence in response to these questions and contend that, in order to adequately answer them, we must redefine the "digital divide" beyond the confines of the access issue. Research and policy debate have been hobbled by a simplistic view of the factors that contribute to technology use and a paucity of information about the relevance of these disparities to the public interest. Access is undeniably important, but the real policy question is how well society will be able to take advantage of the opportunities offered by technology.

An issue definition based primarily on access contains an implicit assumption that the policy problem is affordability rather than *ability* to use technology. Yet certain skills are necessary to exploit the potential of computers, including the ability to use complex software programs or to locate and evaluate information on the web.

Even if evidence demonstrates the existence of an access and skills divide, that is not justification enough for public action. For a condition to qualify as a policy issue rather than a personal concern, there must be something at stake for the larger society. Current Federal Communication Commission chief Michael Powell has dismissed the issue of the digital divide by saying that there is a Mercedes divide as well.[9] If computers and the Internet are just the latest luxury item, or technological toys, little different from microwaves or DVDs, then there is sparse justification for public intervention. What defines the access and skills divides as appropriate issues for public policy are the *uses* of information technology. Computers and the Internet are, among other things, tools for participation in the economy and the political arena. Technology disparities merit policy attention because of their implications for important normative issues such as equality of opportunity and democracy. Information technology also has "positive externalities," or spillover benefits.

Information technology skills and access are "public goods," because, like education and libraries, they are capable of providing positive externalities associated with economic growth and democratic governance. Economists justify government intervention in the market when there are externalities, or effects that ripple beyond the individuals who are directly involved in a transaction. Positive externalities mean that the market, left to its own devices, will likely *under-provide* such commodities. Because individuals fail to "capture" all of the benefits of the knowledge and skills they acquire, they will tend to undervalue them and underinvest from the point of view of society as a whole. Public subsidy or public provision in such cases is more efficient than the market, because governments are able to act in the public interest and to realize the additional social benefits. How then, does society gain from increasing technology use?

Beyond the economic benefits that accrue to individuals when they acquire new skills, a community or a nation with a well-educated workforce is more productive and competitive, particularly within the context of the knowledge-intensive economy that has developed in the advanced capitalist countries over the past few decades. "Human capital"—or "the acquired skills, knowledge, and capacities of human beings"—is a productive resource, as necessary for production as other inputs such as physical capital.[10] Just as widespread education raises the level of human capital in the economy, so do critical technology skills that are increasingly important throughout the economy.

Likewise, there are positive externalities to be found in the political arena. An educated and informed citizenry is more interested in and knowledgeable about political issues and is thus more likely to vote, voice opinions, organize, volunteer on behalf of the community, run for office, and govern. Political knowledge and the skills to participate not only empower individuals, but are also necessary for the functioning of a democracy. The "public good" provided the primary rationale for Thomas Jefferson's advocacy of schools as a central feature of a ward system of "little republics"[11] and Horace Mann's campaign for a system of common schools in the nineteenth century.[12] Similar arguments have supported the establishment of public libraries since Benjamin Franklin. Like schools and libraries, the Internet has become a resource for political and civic information— from campaign to government websites. In addition, computers and the Internet may become increasingly important for access to the political process, as suggested by recent experiments with Internet voting and electronic town meetings (see chapter 5).

Beyond the potential for social gain through public support for information technology access and skills, we believe that there is also a compelling argument for attention to these issues based on equity. The idea of equal opportunity (if not equal results) resonates powerfully in the American polity, from the Horatio Alger myth to the struggles of the civil rights movement. Most frequently, this ideal is evoked in connection with the ability to compete economically, but equal opportunity also applies to the exercise of the rights of democratic citizenship. Universal access to public education has been called "America's answer to the European welfare state," emphasizing preparation for economic and political participation rather than equitable outcomes.[13] Although the United States provides fewer redistributive social programs than most other developed nations, it was the first to guarantee free public education at both the primary and secondary levels. To the extent that computers and the Internet offer tools for economic self-sufficiency and political engagement, the price of unequal technology skills and access may be to perpetuate or even widen existing social inequities. Robert Putnam argues that disparities in information technology represent a "cyberapartheid" that diminishes the store of bridging social capital necessary for connecting disparate elements of society.[14]

Our goal, then, is to explore these multiple dimensions of disparities in information technology—to establish whether in fact significant technology divides exist for access, skills, economic opportunity, and democratic participation. The next section discusses our research design, the analytical methods we use, and the advantages of these approaches.

Methodology

In view of our task of exploring multiple divides, we chose to examine the skills, attitudes, and experiences of the individuals who were most likely to be affected by a lack of computer access and skills. Three features of our study improve upon previous research on the digital divide. First, our study draws upon a unique source of data, a survey that features a broader set of questions relevant to all four divides rather than merely technology access or use. Second, our data are derived from a larger sample of low-income respondents than most information technology surveys (other than the very large sample studies used by the NTIA), which increases confidence in our findings. We drew one sample from high-poverty areas and another from the general population. Third, we use multiple controls in analyzing the data, which allow us to sort out which factors account for observed differences and which are statistically significant. Our findings on access contradict some previous studies that have used simpler techniques.[15] Although we use more rigorous methods, we report most results using probabilities, so that no statistical background is required for readers.

Collecting the Data

Our primary source of data is a national telephone survey conducted in June and July 2001 by Kent State University's Computer Assisted Telephone Interviewing (CATI) lab in the Department of Sociology. Respondents were at least twenty-one years of age. One national random sample of 1,190 respondents was drawn from all high-poverty census tracts in the forty-eight contiguous states, excluding Alaska and Hawaii. High-poverty tracts were defined as those with 50 percent or more of the households living at or below 150 percent of the federal poverty level. The response rate for individuals in the high-poverty tracts was 92 percent. Federal data show that telephone service now reaches 94 percent of the population, so telephone surveys are a reasonable methodology for obtaining sample data even in low-income communities.[16] A second national random sample of 655 respondents drawn without regard to the poverty rate of the census tract served as a control group and had a response rate of 88 percent. There were 1,837 valid responses overall.

Telephone numbers were dialed daily through the months of June and July (with 37 days in the field) by trained interviewers. Up to 524 callbacks were attempted to contact potential respondents for the general population sample, and 371 were attempted for the low-income sample. Answering machines were treated as "no answer" and called back on a regular no-answer rotation, a minimum of three hours later. After securing the cooperation of interview subjects, interviewers used CATI systems to administer questions and record responses. The telephone survey included fifty items and averaged 8.5 minutes to complete. The specific wording of each survey question is given in appendix 2.

The process of identifying all high poverty census tracts in the forty-eight states and drawing a separate random sample from them was laborious, which is why few other national surveys pursue such an approach. We believed, however, that such an effort was necessary in this case. Because our survey targeted high-poverty areas, our sample included a relatively large proportion of racial and ethnic minorities, compared to standard surveys. Of the 1,837 respondents, 70 percent were white non-Latino, 19 percent were African American, 9 percent were Latino, and 1.5 percent Asian American. Thus, Latinos and African Americans comprised 28 percent of the sample population, compared to 25 percent of the U.S. population in the 2000 census. Thirty-eight percent of our sample had household incomes below $30,000. This allowed us to make accurate inferences to minority and low-income populations as a whole. The survey generated data that were comparable to large-sample studies, adding to our confidence in the validity of our findings. As shown in the next chapter, our figures closely track the numbers in the large-sample U.S. Department of Commerce study conducted in August of 2001 on parallel questions of access and use, providing further evidence that our sample is a representative one.

Measuring the Divides

To measure the multiple divides, we use various survey responses as the dependent variable or the outcome to be explained.

The access divide. For the access divide, we are interested in access (whether the individual has home access to a computer, home access to the Internet, an e-mail account), the location of computer and Internet use (at home, at work, at the home of a friend or relative, at a library, etc.), and the frequency of use at each location. This gives us a more complete picture than home access alone and allows us to compare patterns of usage by frequency and location.

The skills divide. For the skills divide, we develop two different indices of skill, one for technical competence and one for information literacy. We also explore preferences for assistance (one-on-one help, group instruction, online help, and printed manuals) and attitudes regarding public access such as computer use at libraries or community centers.

The economic opportunity divide. To examine the opportunity divide, we document beliefs about computers and economic advancement and attitudes and experiences for online job search and taking a course online.

The democratic divide. For the democratic divide, we measure attitudes and experiences regarding Internet use for voting, registering to vote, looking up government information, looking up political information, and participating in an electronic town meeting.

Policy recommendations. In our discussion of policy recommendations in the final chapter, we also include attitudes about vouchers and a summary index measuring differences in "digital experience."

Analyzing the Data

In our analysis of the survey data, we begin by listing the simple percentages (or frequencies) for the responses we received, in order to describe overall tendencies. Where we differ from previous studies, however, is our use of a technique called multivariate regression. This widely used statistical method allows us to list a number of "independent variables," or possible explanatory factors for each result (for example, home access), and to identify which are statistically significant predictors for the result (for example, whether education, income, race, gender, and age are related to home access). As we demonstrate in chapter 2, such crucial statistical techniques are lacking in nearly all of the research that has been disseminated on the "digital divide." The independent variables we use vary somewhat based on the research question, but we examine a number of socioeconomic and demographic factors, employment status, and political variables such as partisanship.

Our income measure deserves explanation. We define low-income individuals as having a household income below $30,000, which captures working families of modest means as well as the very poor. There was a very low response rate to questions about income beyond our initial screen of above or below $30,000, which makes it difficult to compare respondents with different levels of poverty. Although ideally we would have liked more specific information about income, we feel that our measure is still a reasonable one, for several reasons. The $30,000 threshold is only about 70 percent of the 2000 median household income of $42,151 reported by the U.S. Census Bureau.[17] In terms of absolute measures of poverty, $30,000 is about 200 percent of the official poverty threshold for a family of three.[18] The federal poverty threshold is calculated by taking a minimal food budget and multiplying that figure by three. The National Academy of Sciences and a number of social scientists have criticized this method as inadequate to account for all a household's needs.[19] Some estimates have placed a more realistic poverty level for a family of four at about $28,000 (in 1999).[20] The Department of Labor has also defined a 2001 "lower living standard income level" for its programs as a little over $30,000 for a family of four in metropolitan areas in either the Northeast or the West.[21]

Our results indicate that many of our "under $30,000" category fall considerably below this threshold. For example, around one-third of survey respondents (32 percent) are currently unemployed, and 87 percent are between twenty-one and sixty-five years of age, indicating most respondents are the working poor or unemployed, not retirees. The fact that nearly two-thirds of our sample was drawn from high-poverty census tracts (with a poverty rate of 50 percent or more) increases the likelihood that many of the individuals listed as having household incomes below $30,000 actually fall below the official poverty level.

To facilitate interpretation of the statistical findings, we present "What Matters" boxes within the text, listing all of the explanatory variables that are statistically significant, without the numbers. For those who are familiar with regression analysis, we also present the multivariate logistic and ordered logistic regression tables in appendix 1. On key questions, we use an additional statistical technique to present our findings. We present probabilities (also in the What Matters boxes) to compare magnitudes for the influence of different explanatory variables—whether income, education, race, age, or gender have a greater impact on access, skills, attitudes, or experience. We convert the regression coefficients from the multivariate models to probabilities using a Monte Carlo simulation technique.[22] As a result, we can report that holding other factors constant, there is a 35 percentage point increase in the probability that individuals with a graduate education will have Internet access, in comparison to individuals with less than a high school diploma. This technique makes the results of the regression models as easy to understand as percentages, requiring no knowledge of statistical methods.

One case study will be briefly reported in the chapter on the democratic divide. The Berkeley, California, city government recently solicited input for revisions to the city plan using an online forum. The Berkeley experience, like an earlier experiment in Santa Monica, California, illustrates that there are numerous challenges in using this form of direct democracy.[23] Ensuring equitable opportunities for participation is only one of these, according to our interviews.

Overview of the Book

The following chapters are organized around four divides, with a concluding chapter that presents some general recommendations for public policy.

Chapter 2, on the access divide reviews the findings of major studies, introduces our own data on the topic and uses multivariate regression to establish the causes of disparities in access. Although previous research has attracted attention to the issue and described trends over the past few years, most studies fall short insofar as they are unable to ascribe with any certainty the causes of inequality in access. We use data from a national study that has tracked Internet access since the mid-1990s and then analyze our own data from 2001, which cover a broader range of questions about access and have a representative sample of low-income individuals. Our findings contradict the conclusions of some previous studies, but affirm that significant disparities in access endure, and are based on multiple factors. Because we use statistical controls, our study can distinguish the influences that matter for the access divide.

Having documented the continued existence of an access divide (using more rigorous analysis), in chapter 3 we venture into largely uncharted territory on the skills divide. We make the case that the Internet requires "information literacy," or the ability to locate and evaluate information through this new medium, in addition to technical competence with hardware and software. There is little research on these topics. Information literacy, however, requires basic literacy, the ability to read and interpret information, as a fundamental prerequisite, and national data show that low levels of literacy are pervasive in the United States. Using our own survey, we describe our findings on technical competence and information literacy. Following our data on the skills divide, we examine the preferences our respondents express for learning new skills and for locations for public access. These preferences are disaggregated by socioeconomic and demographic characteristics, offering some guidance for public policy intended to assist disadvantaged groups in acquiring information-age skills.

The next two chapters of the book shift from describing the boundaries of the access and skills divide to an investigation of their possible consequences. In both chapters, we approach this task by first surveying evidence on the implications of technology disparities and then discussing our data on the attitudes and experiences of our low-income sample. This allows us to study beliefs and needs within different contexts, rather than attitudes about technology in the abstract.

In chapter 4, we examine trends in the "new economy" and find that technology gaps do indeed affect economic opportunity, but often in complex ways. Rapid change may further increase the importance of technology for jobs and economic mobility in the future. Our data on attitudes show widespread belief in a connection between computer skills and economic advancement as well as some unexpected patterns in the groups most likely to perceive technology as economically advantageous. Similar relationships appear in regard to attitudes and experiences with online job searches. Economic advancement is clearly a salient motivation for learning technology skills and using the Internet, for the population as a whole and for some disadvantaged groups in particular.

Chapter 5, on the democratic divide, defines the possibilities for technology in the political sphere, from campaign websites, Internet voting and registration, electronic town meetings, and "e-government," initiatives that place information and services at the disposal of citizens on the web. Scholarly debates tend to either overemphasize or dismiss the role of technology in democratic participation, and the empirical evidence so far is sketchy on many of these issues.[24] Examining attitudes and current use allows us to predict demand for future innovation as well as who is likely to use technology for political participation and who is not. Our assessment is that computers and the Internet promise to increase participation among some groups, while reinforcing or even aggravating disparities in participation for others.

The final chapter summarizes the results for each of the previous chapters and draws some conclusions across the four divides regarding the impact of factors such as race and education. We develop an index of "digital experience" to show some commonalities in who currently uses information technology for economic and political participation. Following a brief survey of current policy efforts, we present a discussion of our recommendations for public policy. Within this context, we include results from the survey on support for vouchers but also discuss other alternatives. The next chapter begins with a reexamination of the access divide, as a first step toward defining the outlines of this multidimensional landscape.

Notes

1. Pippa Norris (2001) provides evidence regarding political participation in a cross-national context, and we emulate her use of the term "democratic divide." We approach the topic somewhat differently, however, with a more extensive examination of disparities in the United States and survey data based on a large sample of low-income and minority respondents.

2. U.S. Department of Commerce 1995.

3. Carvin, Conte, and Gilbert 2001; Puma, Chaplin, and Pape 2000.

4. Hoffman, Novak, and Schlosser (2001, 55) have credited Lloyd Morrisett of the Markle Foundation with coining the term, "digital divide," but Benjamin Compaine (2001, xiv), in the same volume, cites Morrisett's uncertainty about the term's origins.

5. See for example, the most recent NTIA report, U.S. Department of Commerce 2002.

6. See Trotter 2001 for a description of these initiatives. Information on the Digital Divide Network can be found at www.digitaldivide.org.

7. Lacey 2000; Thierer 2000.

8. U.S. Department of Commerce 2002.

9. Shadid 2001.

10. Salamon 1991, 3.

11. Jefferson [1816] 1988.

12. Mann [1839] 1988.

13. Hochschild and Scovronick 2000, 209.

14. Putnam 2000, 175.

15. Nie and Erbring 2000.

16. U.S. Department of Commerce 1995.

17. U.S. Census Bureau 2001.

18. U.S. Census Bureau 2002a.

19. National Academy of Sciences 1996.

20. Uchitelle 1999.

21. See U.S. Department of Labor 2002.

22. See King, Tomz, and Wittenberg 2000. This technique involves calculating the change in the probability of Internet access, for example, that is caused by moving from a variable's minimum to maximum value while simultaneously keeping all other variables set to their mean.

23. Dutton 1999, 184–85.

24. See also Norris 2001.

Chapter 2

The Access Divide

with Ramona McNeal

W hen public officials talk about policy with regard to the digital divide, the topic usually centers on access. During the Clinton administration, policies implemented to address disparities in information technology usage were expressly designed to increase Internet access. Programs such as the Technology Opportunities Program (TOP) under the Department of Commerce and the Community Technology Center (CTC) initiative and the E-Rate administered by the Department of Education were put into place to increase access to disadvantaged groups. When President Bush released his budget proposal for the fiscal year 2003, it called for the termination of both the TOP and CTC initiatives.[1] The reasoning for ending these programs, like the justification for creating them, is based on access. The 2002 Department of Commerce report *A Nation Online: How Americans Are Expanding Their Use of the Internet* argued that these programs had met their goals and that the American public is coming online at a satisfactory rate.[2]

Whereas the Bush administration predicts sunny skies in its digital divide forecasts, others see darker clouds on the information technology horizon. More than 100 groups, including the National Urban League, the National Congress of American Indians, and the American Council of the Blind, came together on Capitol Hill in May 2002 to launch the Digital Empowerment Campaign to oppose Bush's decision to cut the CTC and TOP programs. Joining these groups was a number of lawmakers, including Senator Barbara Mikulski (D-Md.) and Representative Ted Strickland (D-Ohio).

They argue that, although it is true that Americans are getting connected in increasing numbers, there are still gaps in online use based
on race, ethnicity, and income. For example, whereas 60 percent of
the white households had Internet access in 2001, only 34 percent of
African American and 38 percent of Latino households did. In addition, whereas nearly 78 percent of households with income between
$50,000 and $75,000 have Internet access, only 40 percent of those
with household incomes between $20,000 and $25,000 have web
access. Groups protesting proposed cuts in the federal budget fear
that elimination of these programs will make it more difficult to
address inequalities related to technology access.[3]

This chapter presents the findings on access from our low-income
survey and subjects our results to more rigorous analysis than the
methods used in previous studies. We therefore provide more deci-
sive evidence that an access divide in fact exists and is not fading over
time. We review the previous research, the conflicting conclusions,
the shortcomings of various studies, and the advantages of our
approach. We include an original analysis of data from the American
National Election Studies (ANES), which allows us to track the access
divide over time, as well as more detailed evidence from our own July
2001 survey.

Evidence from Prior Research

Although both the Bush administration and members of the Digital
Empowerment Campaign assessed computer access in the United
States using the same report, *A Nation Online: How Americans Are
Expanding Their Use of the Internet,* one saw a glass that is half full
while the other concluded that the access glass is half empty. "Facts"
are often interpreted in starkly different ways in the midst of political battles, of course,[4] but in this case the existing empirical literature
on computer and Internet access is indeed murky and incomplete. *A
Nation Online,* like most studies on Internet access, reports only simple frequencies, or percentages, which tell little about the strength of
the association between variables or the relationship between variables. It is well-known that race, ethnicity, income, and education are
highly correlated, thus simple frequencies or percentages can overestimate the gaps in information technology based on any one of these

factors. African Americans and Latinos, for example, tend to have lower incomes and educational attainment than do whites. The question, then, is whether race is an independent (nonspurious) predictor of access to information technology or whether, for example, education is really driving differences in access.

The overwhelming majority of current studies rely primarily on bar charts based on simple percentages. At most, these reports might examine two variables at a time—for example, African American respondents by income.[5] These approaches are useful for illustrating trends and *suggesting* possible relationships. Descriptive data published by the U.S. Commerce Department and Pew Charitable Trust have served as important indicators of a developing policy problem, thrusting the issue into the public spotlight; however, data of this type are inadequate for making claims about the root causes of the problem and can be open to different interpretations. The methods that have been used to analyze the access divide are insufficient to separate the effects of overlapping influences and to establish with any certainty what factors matter—race, education, income, or all of the above. Our task in this chapter is to sort out the causal determinants in who has access to information technology in the United States. Before discussing our own analyses, we review the evidence presented in major studies, from the U.S. Department of Commerce, the Pew Charitable Trust, academic research, and market surveys.

U.S. Department of Commerce— Reliable Data, No Statistical Controls

A Nation Online is fifth in a series of reports created by the National Telecommunications and Information Administration (NTIA) that examine disparities in usage and access to information technology. The data reported by the NTIA are drawn from survey questions from the U.S. Census Bureau's Current Population Survey (CPS), administered to a large sample of 50,000–60,000 households.[6] When the first NTIA report, *Falling through the Net: A Survey of the "Have Nots" in Rural and Urban America,* was published in 1995, the Internet had not yet gained widespread acceptance and was still mainly a tool for academics and the defense industry.[7] The Internet went unnoticed in this first report, which instead focused on the penetration of telephones, personal computers, and modems. The second

(1998) and third (1999) reports, *Falling through the Net: New Data on the Digital Divide*[8] and *Falling through the Net: Defining the Digital Divide,*[9] measured Internet access, as well as access to computers, and were instrumental in bringing the term "digital divide" into the public consciousness.

The second report found that Americans were in general expanding their access to telecommunication technology such as telephones, computers, and the Internet; however, gaps based on demographic and geographical factors existed. Although differences in access continued based on age, gender, education, rural/urban regions, and single/dual parent households, there were growing disparities based on race, ethnicity, and income when compared to levels from the first report. These differences were particularly acute when examining Internet access and computer ownership. At the time of the first NTIA report (1995), computer ownership among African Americans (10.3 percent) was 16.8 percentage points lower than for whites (27.1 percent). This gap increased to 21.5 percent (40.8 percent for whites and 19.3 percent for African Americans) by the second report in 1998. The difference between white home access (27.1 percent) and Latino home access (12.3 percent) increased from 14.8 percentage points for the 1995 report to 21.4 percent in the second NTIA report (19.4 percent Latino home access).

Like the second report, the third report found that, although Americans were getting more connected, the gaps based on income, education and race/ethnicity were still widening further. During the single year between the second and third reports, the gap between white and African American households in Internet access increased to 37.7 percent. For white and Latino households the disparity in Internet access rose to 37.6 percent. Over the same period, the difference in Internet access between college graduates and those with only a high school degree escalated to 13.2 percent, while the divide between the highest and lowest income levels expanded to 24.3 percent. These findings led the NTIA to conclude that disparities in information technology were based on race and ethnicity as well as education and income.[10]

Although the second and third reports told a story of inequality, the final two reports began to show signs of a narrowing divide. The fourth report (2000), *Falling through the Net: Toward Digital Inclusion,* found that Internet access had increased across all groups and that the gender gap had largely disappeared. Nevertheless, the report also observed that an access divide remained based on income, education, race, ethnicity, age, disabilities, and dual/single parent households. The gap in Internet access between whites (46.1 percent) and African Americans (23.5 percent) was 22.6 percent; similarly, the difference between whites and Latinos (23.6 percent) was 22.5 percent. Although the race and ethnicity gaps had narrowed somewhat, they were still substantial. The difference in Internet access between those with a bachelor's degree (64 percent) and a high school diploma (29.9 percent) was larger still, at 34.1 percent. Most striking was the gap between individuals with a household income greater than $75,000 (77.7 percent) and those with a household income less than $15,000 (12.7 percent), a difference of 65 percentage points.[11]

The final report (2002), *A Nation Online,* again noted increases across all groups and found that urban and rural differences were disappearing.[12] Nevertheless, it reported persistent gaps in "Internet use" based on age, income, education, race, ethnicity, dual/single parent households, and, in particular, mental or physical disabilities. Unlike the other NTIA studies, *A Nation Online* emphasized Internet *use* instead of Internet *access* at home. This measure is different from access in that it includes use of the Internet at work and school rather than only at home, where the divide is greatest. There is nothing inherently wrong, of course, with measuring use, and it is possible to debate whether this is actually a more significant measure than home access. When compared to the access measure, however, Internet use figures can give the impression that technology gaps are narrower than they actually are, especially if frequency of use in locations outside the home is not taken into account.

Because of the large sample sizes of the CPS, the NTIA reports can be used to generalize to the American population. As a government agency, however, the NTIA collects and publishes data rather than models cause-and-effect relationships.

Pew Research Center Surveys— Reliable Data, No Statistical Controls

Like the NTIA, the Pew Research Center began conducting a series of studies on Internet access in 1995. Also like the NTIA reports, these studies were based primarily on descriptive statistics (frequencies and simple percentages) presented as bar charts. The same limitations of the NTIA data analysis apply to the Pew studies, for they cannot sort out the causes of inequities in access to information technology. There is considerable overlap between the findings in the two series of reports. The Pew Research Center found in its *Who's Not Online* report that by spring 2000 gender had reached parity in Internet access but gaps still remained based on income, education, age, race, ethnicity, and geographic location.[13] Although the Pew report found gaps, they were not of the same magnitude as those documented by the NTIA. The NTIA in 2000 reported a 22.6 percent difference between whites and African Americans and a 22.5 percent gap between whites and Latinos in Internet access; the differences for the PEW study were only 14 percent and 6 percent. The NTIA also reported a 34.1 percent disparity based on educational attainment (between those with high school and college degrees), whereas the Pew study found a larger (41 percent) difference. The 2000 Pew Internet and American Life Project report, "African-Americans and the Internet," concluded that, when survey results were broken down by income and education, differences in access based on race still remained.[14] The 2000 NTIA report reached the same conclusion for both race and ethnicity. Some research has suggested that racial and ethnic disparities in Internet access may be partly due to the fact that minorities have different information and content needs that the Internet is not meeting.[15] Like the NTIA studies, the Pew surveys include representative samples that can be used to draw generalizations about the American public (but not specifically the poor), but the data gauge trends rather than trying to isolate explanations for the trends.

Academic Studies—Older Data, Some Analysis with Statistical Controls

Academic studies have differed in their assessment of which factors are responsible for disparities in access, demonstrating how much research methods influence findings. Hoffman, Novak, and Schlosser conclude that race, as well as income and education, matters, but their study is limited by the absence of statistical controls.[16] Neu, Anderson, and Bikson[17] and Wilhelm[18] conducted two of the rare studies using multivariate regression, which controls for multiple influences. Neu, Anderson, and Bikson used the 1993 and 1997 CPS and logistic regression to predict access to a home computer and e-mail use. They found that income, education, race, and ethnicity were important factors for both. Computer access and e-mail use were greatest among Asian Americans and whites who were more affluent and more educated. Age and region also played a part in determining access, but to a lesser extent, with the young more likely to have a computer and e-mail access.[19] Because of their use of more sophisticated methods, Neu, Anderson, and Bikson provide a more complete picture of the digital divide than can be puzzled together from more recent studies of access. Nevertheless, this study was based on older data that are limited in their ability to predict current trends in access to information technology.

Wilhelm, like Neu, Anderson, and Bikson, used multivariate statistics (logistic regression) and based his research on the 1994 CPS to examine home computer and modem ownership. The interpretations and validity of the research, however, are limited by errors in the data analysis that have the effect of obscuring differences based on race and ethnicity.[20] Not surprisingly, Wilhelm discovered little racial or ethnic influence. In addition, the study relies on older data.

In one of the best-known academic studies, Nie and Erbring found that only education and age matter in the digital divide.[21] Their study was based on data collected in December 1999 through a national survey of 4,113 individuals in a 2,689-household panel. Each member of a panel household filled out separate questionnaires. Because this study focused on online behavior and the survey was conducted over the Internet, all respondents (even those without previous access) were provided with a *WebTV* set-top box and free Internet access and e-mail accounts. The results on Internet use presented in the study, however, were based solely on participants who had previous access.[22] This survey design, while unique, violates the assumption of independence underlying statistical methods by allowing more than one member of a household to participate in the study. Using multiple members of the same household biases the sample so that it is not representative of the population as a whole. If survey respondents are not randomly selected, using statistics to draw conclusions that apply to the whole population is questionable in terms of reliability. Again, only simple frequencies and percentages are reported in the study.

Market Research Surveys—Questionable Data and Analysis

Whereas the NTIA reports and Pew Research have found enduring gaps in Internet access, other studies report conflicting findings. Marketing research firms (e.g., Forrester Research Inc., Cheskin Research) provide their clients with studies that show how best to take advantage of this new market. Their research does not always coincide with the findings of government, foundation, or academic studies. In particular, some surveys from marketing research firms have suggested that the divide based on race has been overstated. For example, a Forrester study based on more than 80,000 mail surveys found that Latino households were more likely to be online than white households. The finding that Latino households are online more than whites directly contradicts the results of the NTIA and Pew Research surveys. The Forrester study also found that income played the greatest role in promoting Internet access, although age, education, and technology optimism are also important factors in determining access. The study suggested that, while African Americans lagged behind in Internet access, it was because of disparities in income and not racial factors.[23] To evaluate the validity of these findings, it is important to know the response rate of the mail survey and the statistical methods on which the conclusions were based. A low response rate, which is common in mail surveys, can bias the findings. Those who take the time to send back the survey may only be those who are already using the Internet and are most interested in the topic. Neither the response rate nor methodology is apparent from the report, making it difficult to assess the validity of the findings.

This pinpoints one of the differences between research that meets academic standards and those of market research. Scholarly research requires that statistical methods are made public, explained in detail, and that the data used are available so that others may attempt to replicate and evaluate the validity of findings. Otherwise, it is impossible to know how trustworthy the findings are. The market surveys do not meet these standards of public scrutiny. Government agencies (such as the Bureau of the Census, which conducted research for the NTIA) and studies funded by major foundations generally observe the standards of academic research. Government agencies aim to provide information about important policy issues but often do not conduct advanced statistical analysis to draw cause-and-effect relationships.

Strange results and methodological flaws in market research might be of little concern if the only audience for these findings was companies that contracted with these firms; however, this less rigorous and transparent research is often publicized in the press or books. The volume edited by Benjamin Compaine and published by MIT Press includes market surveys on the same footing as government or academic studies. The editor, in fact, argues that Forrester, Cheskin, and the academic study by Nie and Erbring, which concluded that race was not a factor, are more "sophisticated" than the NTIA and the Hoffman, Novak, and Schlosser studies that found that race did matter.[24]

Summary of the Previous Research

Our review of the research has found that a number of surveys have been conducted exploring demographic and geographic factors that may impact computer and Internet access. All of the eight studies summarized found enduring gaps in Internet access based on education and age. Seven of the eight reported that income played an important role in promoting technology access. The findings were mixed in terms of whether factors such as race and ethnicity were important, with four of the eight studies reporting access gaps based on race and ethnicity. None of the studies found gaps in technology access based on gender, but other factors cited in regard to computer access include dual/single parent households, mental or physical disabilities, geographic location, employment status, and optimism about technology.

The Need for Reliable Data and Analysis with Statistical Controls

While the fast-changing population of Internet users creates an obstacle for making predictions, the greatest weakness related to previous research has been the lack of appropriate statistical methods, specifically statistical controls. Most studies have simply described the percentage of a certain group that has computer or Internet access. Even studies that use cross-tabulation tables to report the relationship between two variables (for example race and income) can be deceptive. Looking at differences across only one or two variables does not permit the researcher to control for the effect of other related factors. Many demographic factors, such as income and education, are inter-related. If you examine them one at a time, the differences found may be in reality attributable to other related factors. The independent effects of race, ethnicity, income, education, age, gender, and employment status can be found only by using an appropriate statistical method, such as multivariate regression.

In an attempt to address some of the weaknesses of previous research, this chapter will use two different surveys to explore the influence of a variety of factors on information technology access. First, we examine broad trends in our own 2001 survey data, using simple percentages. Second, we analyze data on Internet access using information drawn from the 1996, 1998, and 2000 ANES survey. The ANES is a nationwide, large-scale study that conducts in-person and telephone surveys using randomly selected respondents. The ANES allows us to examine Internet access over time, while our survey includes more specific questions about access to varying forms of information technology and also includes a representative sample of low-income respondents. In addition to using complementary data sources, we employ a more accurate methodology to analyze the data. Simple percentages are supplemented by multivariate regression procedures and a Monte Carlo simulation technique that estimates probabilities and predicts the likelihood of information technology access.[25]

Low-Income Survey: Patterns of Access and Use

Frequencies provide descriptive trends and a first cut at the data in terms of understanding who does and does not have access to information technology. Sixty-one percent of our respondents reported having access to a home computer, and 54 percent reported having home Internet access. This closely tracks the figures on Internet use for the U.S. Department of Commerce study conducted in September 2001.[26] Compared to the 61 percent of respondents who have home computer access, 58 percent had an e-mail address through which they can send or receive e-mail. Only a small percentage of respondents (14 percent) said they had high-speed Internet access. We also included more detailed questions on alternative ways to access information technology. This is especially important for low-income respondents who do not have a computer or Internet access at home.

The survey allowed respondents the opportunity to identify multiple locations for access to computers and the Internet. Almost equal percentages of respondents used a computer at home (54 percent) and at work (49 percent). Of employed respondents, however, 65 percent used the computer at work. Relatively small percentages of respondents (15 percent) used the computer at a school or a public library. Yet more than a quarter of those surveyed used the computer at a friend or relative's house (26 percent). This suggests the interpersonal potential of information technology use, perhaps for entertainment, information search, or informal instruction.

A parallel story emerges when examining venues for Internet access. Compared to the 51 percent of respondents who actually used the Internet at home, 34 percent used the Internet at work (45 percent of employed respondents used the Internet at work), while close to the same number use the Internet at a school (11 percent) or a public library (10 percent). Twenty percent used the Internet at a friend or relative's house, which is double the rate of Internet use at libraries and schools. For the general population, usage of information technology at home, however, far outweighed usage at other locations, even work. This finding demonstrates the importance of measuring home Internet access rather than lumping together Internet access at home and other locations. Home access allows more privacy and greater flexibility in terms of length of use and round-the-clock availability.

How do these figures change if we examine the answers given by people who do *not* have a computer at home? Do more of these individuals use computers at other places? Of the 710 respondents without a home computer, 30 percent use the computer at work, 9 percent at school, and 13 percent at the library. Twenty-four percent used a computer at a friend's house. These frequencies are comparable to those for the overall population. The data suggest that patterns of computer use outside the home do not differ significantly among those with and without a home computer. Individuals without a home computer are not using public access more than those with home access. The Internet is used even *less* outside the home by those without a home Internet connection. Of the 841 respondents without Internet access at home, 17.5 percent indicated they use the Internet at work, 7 percent at school, 9 percent at the library and 16 percent at a friend's house. These figures are *lower* than the percentages for the overall population. The data show that work or the homes of friends and relatives are the most common venues to access information technology outside of the home, regardless of home access.

Home and work are clearly associated with more frequent access to information technology than a friend or relative's house, schools, or public libraries. We asked respondents about the number of times they used computers and the Internet at varying locations. When asked, "Last month, how often did you use a computer at home," 14 percent reported low usage (1–10 times), 20 percent moderate usage (11–30 times), and 17 percent high usage (31–100 times), while 5 percent reported very high usage (more than 100 times). Very high frequency of computer use was more likely to take place at work rather than at home: 8 percent reported low use at work (1–10 times), 12 percent moderate use (11–30 times), 17 percent high use (31–100 times), and 12 percent very high use of over 100 times. In contrast, frequency of access was much lower at a friend or relative's house: 22 percent reported low use (1–10 times), 2 percent moderate use (11–30 times), and less than 1 percent of the respondents high or very high use at a friend or relative's house. Frequency of access at public libraries was even lower. Only 12 percent reported low usage, 1.5 percent moderate usage, and less than 1 percent high or very high usage. Although friends, relatives, and libraries may provide exposure to information technology, work or home access is associated with consistent use.

Exploring Patterns of Access with Statistical Controls

The descriptive statistics presented in the last section give us a picture of current access and use but tell us little about the causes of disparities or the development of trends. Our survey provides data from a single point in time. To assess the validity of our low-income survey data and to understand changes over time, we analyze access to information technology drawing on the 1996, 1998, and 2000 ANES. This large-scale, nationwide study selects respondents randomly for in-person and telephone surveys. The ANES is conducted every two years and provides one of the most comprehensive sources of data regarding popular attitudes toward government. Beginning in 1996, the ANES also began collecting data on Internet access and use. For the remainder of this chapter, we use multivariate statistics to ascertain which factors are statistically significant when we control for other possible explanations.

Before presenting our findings, a few words are necessary to describe our model. The dependent variable—the result that we want to explain—is Internet access.[27] The independent variables—the factors that potentially influence Internet access—are individual-level attitudinal and demographic factors suggested by the findings of previous studies and the fifth report (2002) of the U.S. Department of Commerce series, *A Nation Online: How Americans Are Expanding Their Use of the Internet.*[28] This most recent installment of the Department of Commerce's digital divide series indicates that, although Internet access has been increasing for all groups, there are still significant gaps based on race, ethnicity, age, and, in particular, income and education.

In our analysis of the ANES, personal income in 1996 and 1998 is measured on a 24-point ordinal scale, where 1 indicates annual family income ranging from $0 to $2,999 and 24 indicates that annual family income is $105,000 or more. In 2000, income is measured on a 22-point scale, where 1 indicates annual family income ranging from $0 to $4,999 and 22 indicates that annual family income is $200,000 or more. Education is measured on a seven-point ordinal scale, with a "dummy" variable for gender, where respondents are coded 1 for female and 0 for male. (Dummy variables are used for gender, race, ethnicity, partisanship, and income. This means that they are coded as categories, with female, African American, Latino, Asian American, Democrat, Republican, and those with an annual income less than $30,000 coded 1 and 0 otherwise.) To control for race and ethnicity, variables for African Americans, Asian Americans, and Latinos were coded 1 and 0 otherwise, with non-Latino whites as the reference group. Age was measured in years. Because we also discuss political participation in chapter 5, we introduce partisanship in the analysis. Chew has found that, when individuals are interested in the political process, they seek out greater levels of media coverage of elections to become better informed.[29] Strongly partisan individuals may also be motivated to gain access to the Internet, so we measure the strength of partisan identification as well. A seven-point scale measures partisanship (1 = strong Democrat to 7 = strong Republican). A series of dummy variables are used to account for political attitudes, including strong Democrat, strong Republican, and pure independent.

The Findings: ANES Data

By examining Internet access over time using statistical controls, we discover some unexpected patterns. One of the most stable findings, shown in table A2.2, is that the young are significantly more likely to have access to the Internet, when we control for other factors. Although the young are more likely to have Internet access, they also tend to have lower incomes. Previous research has modeled the relationship between income and computer and Internet access using a simple linear relationship—that is, as income increases, Internet access increases.[30] We find the relationship between income and Internet access to be more complex and more accurately measured by a nonlinear (quadratic) model, which we explain below.

Because young people were the first to embrace the Internet, regardless of income, when going online was a relatively new phenomenon, low-income individuals were actually more likely to have Internet access in 1996 and 1998. Thus, in 1996 and 1998 the low-income groups (which often included the young and students) and upper-income groups tended to have the highest access to the Internet. By 2000 the number of Internet users had expanded sufficiently that the expected relationship of increased income is associated with more Internet access.[31] In the analysis of the low-income data in the next section, we model a linear relationship between income and Internet access, reflecting this finding.

Across the years, individuals with more education are more likely to have access to the Internet, holding other factors constant. In 1998, females are less likely to have Internet access than males, but this relationship does not hold in 1996 and 2000. There is evidence that strong Republicans are more likely to have Internet access and strong Democrats significantly less, confirming previous research.[32] We will return to this issue in the chapter on the democratic divide. The other notable finding is that African Americans have significantly lower access to the Internet in both 1998 and 2000 compared to whites.[33] Our analysis of the ANES survey is fairly consistent with government reports that are not based on multivariate statistics and earlier studies based on e-mail access alone.[34] The main difference we discovered was that relationship between income and access was complex at the beginning of the Internet's diffusion, because of the number of students and other young people who adopted the technology early on. A more straightforward relationship between income and access has developed over time.

Low-Income Survey Data

The ANES survey data, however, do not include a representative sample of the poor or of African American and Latino populations. Accurately measuring the experiences of these important populations is necessary to sufficiently define the access divide. The ANES data also do not include measures of access such as e-mail. Do the same demographic patterns associated with Internet access using the ANES data appear in our national representative sample?

Table A2.3 uses logistic regression and multivariate analysis based on low-income survey data to examine factors associated with computer use and Internet access. We present three different analyses, based on the questions, "Do you personally have a home computer?" "Do you have an e-mail address with which you can send and receive e-mail?" and "Do you have access to the Internet from home?"[35]

Consistent with the analysis based on the ANES data, explanatory variables include gender, race, ethnicity, partisanship, income, and education. For race and ethnicity whites were the reference, or left-out, group that was not coded. For partisanship, those without strong partisan identification—independents—were the reference group that was not included. Education was measured on a five-point scale with responses ranging from 1 (less than a high school degree) to 5 (postgraduate work). Age was recorded in years. We present the results of our regression analysis in the following What Matters box. The factors listed are those that are statistically significant, when controlling for other explanations.

As in previous research, the poor, the less educated, and the old were significantly less likely to have a home computer, an e-mail address, or Internet access. Unlike the ANES data, which include

WHAT MATTERS

Who Is Least Likely to Have Internet Access at Home?

Poor
Less-educated
Old
Democrats
Latinos
African Americans

Who Is Least Likely to Have an E-Mail Address?[a]

Poor
Less-educated
Old
Females
Latinos
African Americans

Who Is Least Likely to Have a Home Computer?[b]

Poor
Less-educated
Old
Latinos
African Americans

Note: The only statistically significant differences are the ones reported above (see table A2.3). When multivariate regression is used, these are the variables that matter, holding other factors constant.

[a]Republicans are statistically more likely to have an e-mail address than independents, but Democrats are not statistically less likely to have an e-mail address.

[b]Republicans are statistically more likely than independents to have a home computer, but Democrats are not.

small samples of racial and ethnic minorities, our data indicate that *both* African Americans and Latinos were significantly less likely to have home computers, e-mail addresses, or Internet access than whites, after controlling for socioeconomic conditions. Findings from the low-income sample demonstrate that race and ethnicity clearly matter in the access divide, even after accounting for variations in income and education. Asian Americans and whites were found to have comparable access. These findings also provide evidence that partisanship is an important factor in measuring the access divide. Republicans were more likely to have an e-mail address and home computers than the reference group (independents), while Democrats were less likely to have Internet access than those without strong partisan ties.

To facilitate interpretation of the statistical findings, our results for home Internet access—arguably the most important of the information technology access variables—were converted to expected probabilities using a Monte Carlo simulation technique.[36] This allows us to compare the magnitude of differences, for example, whether education or income is more important, even if they are both statistically significant. The results are easy to understand, because they resemble simple percentages. It is important to remember, however, that these are probabilities based on regression models rather than percentages. In other words, a 17 percent difference based on race should be read as a 17 percentage point difference in the probability that African Americans will have Internet access, compared to the probability for whites, holding all other factors constant.

The estimates provide an interesting comparison of access based on income, education, gender, race, age, and partisanship. We calculate the change in the probability of access caused by moving from a variable's minimum to maximum value while simultaneously keeping all other variables set to their mean (or the change in the probability of home Internet access when moving from the 1 to 0 category for dichotomous, or dummy, variables).

The simulations show that income plays an important role in determining home Internet access, controlling for other factors, including education, age, race, ethnicity, gender, and partisanship. All else equal, individuals in the lower income category had a 39 percent probability of having Internet access, compared to those in the highest income group, who had a 63 percent probability of enjoying home Internet access, a difference of 24 percentage points.

Education was important as well. Holding other factors constant, college graduates were 21 percent more likely to have home Internet access than those with only a high school diploma; those with some graduate education were 35 percent more likely to have Internet access than those without a high school degree. Of respondents with some graduate education, 71 percent had access to the Internet at

WHAT MATTERS

Who Is Least Likely to Have Internet Access at Home?

Poor (39% for low-income vs. 63% for high-income)—24-point difference

Old (43% for 61-year-olds vs. 67% for 28-year-olds)—24-point difference

Less-educated (44% for high school graduates vs. 65% for college graduates)—21-point difference

African Americans (37% vs. 54% for whites)—17-point difference

Latinos (41% vs. 54% for whites)—13-point difference

Democrats (54% vs. 64% for Republicans)—10-point difference

Note: Estimates are based on a hypothetical respondent who is female, white, and independent, with values for education, age, and income set at their mean. The only statistically significant differences are the ones reported above (see table A2.3). We have calculated the probability of access, holding other factors constant.

home, compared to 65 percent of college graduates, 54 percent of individuals with some college, 44 percent of high school graduates and 36 percent of respondents without a high school degree. Education and income emerged as important factors in the access divide, consistent with other studies, even in multivariate statistical analyses.

As the earlier analysis of the ANES data showed, age continues to be an important factor. The simulations show a 24 percent increased probability of having access for twenty-eight-year-olds (one standard deviation below the mean) in comparison to individuals who are sixty-one years of age (one standard deviation above the mean). For the young, the likelihood of having Internet access from home was 67 percent, all else equal, compared to older respondents, for whom there was a 43 percent likelihood of having home Internet access. Holding other demographic and attitudinal factors constant, differences based on gender were not statistically significant.

Contradicting other reports that find only education and age matter in the digital divide, we find that race and ethnicity clearly do matter, though somewhat less than education and income.[37] Asian Americans had the highest predicted probability of Internet access (72 percent), with whites significantly behind (54 percent). Latinos trail whites (41 percent), and the probability of having home Internet access is lowest for African Americans (37 percent). The difference in the probability of home Internet access between Asian Americans and African Americans is 35 percent. Even after holding constant socioeconomic status, some racial and ethnic minorities (African Americans and Latinos) are significantly less likely to have access to the Internet at home than whites and Asian Americans.

The findings for partisanship were mixed. Democrats were less likely to have Internet access (54 percent) than Republicans (64 percent) and independents (58 percent). Because individuals with Republican partisanship are 10 percentage points more likely to have access to the Internet at home than Democrats, this may have some influence on policy. Republicans may be less concerned about issues such as the access divide, for example, or may be more interested in issues such as e-government, given their more wired constituency.

Conclusion

The aims of this chapter have been both descriptive and analytical. Our low-income sample offers a detailed picture of computer and Internet access for disadvantaged groups. Several trends are visible. Most Americans use computers and the Internet at home or work, and a quarter use computers at a friend or relative's house. A much smaller percentage (about 15 percent) use public access services at libraries. The percentage of people who use computers in places outside the home is similar for both those with and without home access, and in fact those lacking a home connection are *less* likely to use the Internet in other places such as libraries. This suggests a lack of interest or a dearth of knowledge and skill regarding the Internet. Frequent use of computers and the Internet occurs at work or at home. Information technology use in other places tends to be sporadic. These simple percentages demonstrate the significance of home access but can tell us little about what influences access.

With the proliferation of sophisticated statistical analyses in the social sciences, it is surprising to find the research on such a well-publicized policy issue dominated by descriptive data. Although an extensive number of surveys on information technology access and use have been conducted by government agencies, nonprofit organizations, and market research firms, few studies report findings based on multivariate regression that can isolate the effect of specific factors on who has access to computers and the Internet. Contradictory findings provide ammunition for both sides as debates rage on in Washington, D.C., the policy community, and academic circles about whether an access divide really exists.[38] Using two sources of data, a representative sample of low-income respondents, and multivariate methods, we find unequal access to the Internet over a period of years and continuing inequities for the Internet, e-mail, and computer ownership. Our analysis of the ANES data over time demonstrates that gender disparities for computer and Internet access have faded. Statistically significant differences still exist in e-mail access, and perhaps this can be explained by differences in jobs. The complex relationship between income and age that existed when young people were among the earliest adopters of the Internet has given way as income has increased in importance. The ANES data show that African Americans are statistically less likely to have access, but the more representative sample in our survey shows that this is true for Latinos as well.

Table 2.1 compares the reported gaps in access to the Internet based on race, ethnicity, education, and income from the NTIA 2000 survey,[39] Pew Research 2000 survey,[40] and analysis of our low-income survey (Tolbert, Stansbury, and Mossberger 2001). While Pew and the NTIA report only simple percentages, our analysis reports expected probabilities based on a multivariate regression analysis that controls for correlation, or overlap, between factors such as race, education, and income.

Although the NTIA survey overestimates racial disparities in Internet access between African Americans and whites, Pew underestimates the racial divide. Our data and analysis suggest that, after controlling for other factors, whites are 17 percentage points more likely to have Internet access than African Americans. In measuring the ethnicity gap, we again estimate a middle position, lower than the NTIA survey and higher than the Pew Research survey. All else equal, we find that whites are 13 percentage points more likely to have Internet access than Latinos.

Because simple percentages tend to exaggerate, or overestimate, the true relationships, our analysis reveals that the education gap is smaller than that reported by Pew and NTIA, but is still substantial and larger than disparities in access based on ethnicity or race. Indi-

Table 2.1
Measuring the Access Divide

Internet Access	Department of Commerce/NTIA Survey[a] (%)	Pew Research Survey[b] (%)	Low-Income Survey[c] (%)
Race gap (African American vs. white)	22.6	14	17
Ethnicity gap (Latino vs. white)	22.5	6	13
Education gap (high school diploma vs. college degree)	34.1	41	21
Income Gap (below $30,000 vs. above $30,000)	39	34	24

Sources: [a] U.S. Department of Commerce 2000b; [b] Pew Research Center 2000; [c] Tolbert, Stansbury, and Mossberger 2001.

Notes: For the low-income survey, data are predicted probabilities based on multivariate regression. Data reported on income gaps for NTIA and Pew are estimates because income is not measured in exactly the same intervals in the three surveys.

viduals with a college degree are 21 percentage points more likely to have Internet access than those with only a high school diploma. Finally, all three studies report enduring gaps between the affluent and poor. Holding other demographic factors constant, we estimate that individuals with incomes above $30,000 are 24 percentage points more likely to have Internet access than those with incomes below $30,000. Our findings are consistent with those reported by the other studies.

The striking result is that all three studies based on different survey data and statistical methods report persistent gaps in access to the Internet based on race, ethnicity, education, and income. This is so even for the most recent data, which have been heralded by the Bush administration as evidence that the digital divide is vanishing and insignificant. The data reveal that a "digital divide" in terms of information technology access is an undeniable reality. Even as more Americans purchase computers and flock online, most of the disparities that emerged during the latter half of the 1990s remain.

Notes

1. Benner 2002, 1.
2. U.S. Department of Commerce 2002.
3. Wright 2002, 1–2.
4. Stone 2002, chap. 13; see also Mossberger 2000, 156.
5. Hoffman, Novak, and Schlosser 2000.
6. U.S. Department of Labor 2002 and U.S. Department of Commerce 2002.
7. U.S. Department of Commerce 1995.
8. U.S. Department of Commerce 1998.
9. U.S. Department of Commerce 1999.
10. U.S. Department of Commerce 1999, 8.
11. U.S. Department of Commerce 2000b. For the racial gap see p. 98; for the educational gap see p. 99; and for the income gap see p. 8.
12. U.S. Department of Commerce 2002.
13. Pew Research Center 2000, 5.
14. Pew Internet and American Life Project 2000, 5.
15. Novak, Hoffman, and Venkatesh 1997, 3; Hoffman, Novak, and Schlosser 2000.
16. Hoffman, Novak, and Schlosser 2000.
17. Neu, Anderson, and Bikson 1999.
18. Wilhelm 2000.
19. Neu, Anderson, and Bikson 1999, 146–48. The authors used logistic regression because they constructed dummy variables for age, gender, race, ethnicity, income, and region (urban, rural, and suburban).
20. Unlike most studies, Wilhelm (2000) included two variables for white (non-Latino) in his analysis: (1) a dummy variable for ethnicity coded 1 for non-Latino and 0 otherwise and (2) a series of dummy variables for race that included white. This dummy variable coding of race/ethnicity creates a situation of near perfect multicollinearity, which makes it impossible to determine the impact of race or ethnicity on access to a home computer or modem. In addition to the dummy variable for white, Wilhelm also included dummy variables for African American, Asian American, and Native American respondents, leaving "other race" as the reference group for race. Given that very few individuals would have been in the reference group, the race variables also suffer from near perfect multicollinearity. Multicollinearity is a violation of the assumptions of linear regression that can lead to invalid findings.

21. Nie and Erbring 2000.

22. Nie and Erbring 2000, 5.

23. Walsh, Gazala, and Ham 2001, 279–84.

24. Compaine 2001, 267.

25. King, Tomz, and Wittenberg 2000.

26. Our figures fall near the data for September 2001 cited by the NTIA. The NTIA reported 66 percent and 54 percent for computer and Internet *use* by individuals, and 57 and 51 percent for household ownership of computers and home Internet access, respectively. Our data for individual home computer and Internet access are within the standard margin of error of ±4 points in comparison to the NTIA's reported household data (U.S. Department of Commerce 2002).

27. Because Internet access is measured by a dummy variable, with Internet access coded 1 and 0 otherwise, logistic regression coefficients are reported in table A2.2.

28. U.S. Department of Commerce 2002.

29. Chew 1994.

30. Neu, Anderson, and Bikson 1999; Department of Commerce 2002.

31. We measure income by including an additional squared term (income multiplied by income) to model a quadratic equation.

32. For similar findings, see Bucy 2000. This does not, however, match the prediction that all strong partisans are likely to have access, as Chew's (1994) findings on other media suggest.

33. Recent research based on the CPS suggests that Asian Americans have higher Internet access than whites (U.S. Department of Commerce 2002).

34. Neu, Anderson, and Bikson 1999.

35. We create three models with the binary dependent variables for home computer access, e-mail, and home Internet access. The dummy variables are coded 1 for access to technology, and 0 for no access. Since the dependent variables are binary, our estimates are based on logistic regression.

36. King, Tomz, and Wittenberg 2000.

37. Nie and Ebring 2000.

38. See Compaine 2001.

39. U.S. Department of Commerce 2000b.

40. Pew Research Center 2000.

Chapter 3

The Skills Divide

Although there have been many reports and studies of the state of access to technology and the Internet, few studies, and none with the scope of the one presented here, have addressed the state of computer-related skills. Two distinct concepts describe the knowledge and skills needed to use information technology effectively. *Technical competencies* are the skills needed to operate hardware and software, such as typing, using a mouse, and giving instructions to the computer to sort records a certain way. *Information literacy* is the ability to recognize when information can solve a problem or fill a need and to effectively employ information resources. Information literacy is needed to navigate the Internet for work, school, political information, medical information, news, entertainment, and other purposes. Both technical competency and information literacy are needed to fully exploit the potential of information technology, although there are a number of computer applications that only require technical competence. Computers and the Internet are more than data storage or communication devices. They are gateways to a seemingly limitless but complex array of information sources of varied uses and quality.

The data from our survey indicate that the technology skills divide is quite pronounced for many groups. The lack of fundamental technology-related skills—such as using a mouse and typing, using e-mail, locating information on the web, and using word processing and spreadsheet programs—is a clear indicator of the need for policy attention to this issue. The acquisition of skills such as technical competence and information literacy may be particularly problematic for some individuals, however, in particular those who lack basic literacy.

This chapter also discusses the preferences for acquiring these skills expressed by survey respondents. Public policy to some extent has supported public libraries and community technology centers as instructional providers for technology as well as locations for public access; however, public libraries and other providers need guidance in the selection of instructional methods. Do those who need to learn how to use a keyboard or a mouse prefer one-on-one instruction? Do those who need to learn how to search for information on the web prefer group instruction? Our survey findings provide some answers to these questions and assist instructional providers in using their resources advantageously.

Because public access can potentially play an important role in addressing the skills divide, we also explore attitudes about public access locations. In the previous chapter, we found that only a small percentage of the population has used libraries for public access and that such use has been almost equally modest even among those who have no computer or Internet access at home. Possible explanations for this finding are that libraries are are not frequented by disadvantaged groups who lack home access, because they are inconvenient or are viewed as unwelcoming or irrelevant to such groups. In this chapter, we explore attitudes about other possible public access sites as well as attitudes about libraries. Along with the data on instructional preferences, our findings on public access offer concrete guidance for policy addressing the skills divide.

This chapter serves as further argument against those who say that the gap is shrinking. If some individuals cannot use computer technology, then all the access in the world will do no good. Further, if people cannot find the assistance they need to use the technology, then access alone does little to alleviate the problem.

Skills for the Information Age

The National Academy of Sciences has declared that for individuals to "participate intelligently and thoughtfully in the world around them," they need the ability to evaluate and select technological solutions to problems.[1] Their definition of "technological literacy" is a far-ranging one, well beyond the more circumscribed set of digital skills that we are concerned with in this chapter.[2] Yet the academy's appeal underscores technology use as an intrinsic need in modern society.

Technical competence and information literacy, though linked, represent distinct skill sets within this overarching idea of technological literacy. As skill sets, they should transcend operating system platforms, software programs, computer makes and models, and database interfaces.

Technical Competence

Technical competence is the ability to operate a computerized or electronic device. For example, using word processing software requires technical competencies such as initiating a file; inputting, formatting, and outputting data; and managing the file itself.

Little research addresses the extent of technical competence among Americans, particularly among groups that are disadvantaged in terms of home access. Both the Pew Internet and American Life project and the Commerce Department's NTIA reports have documented some of the ways in which the Internet is used, from which we can extrapolate technical competencies. In a 2001 survey, Pew found that 45 percent of Americans used e-mail, 36 percent used the Internet for product and service information, 39 percent made online purchases, and 35 percent searched for health information on the Internet.[3] The U.S. Department of Commerce has collected data on the prevalence of different tasks in the workplace by occupational category that suggest demand for certain competencies.[4] For example, managers and professionals were found to use the Internet and e-mail at a 66.8 percent rate, word processing and desktop publishing at a 63.2 percent rate, and spreadsheets and databases at a 56.6 percent rate.[5] The extent of competency was not addressed in either study—whether respondents who used e-mail could apply filters, organize folders of mail, and open e-mail attachments, for example, or whether they sometimes needed help with word processing or spreadsheets. Nevertheless, simply being able to perform these tasks implies a certain level of technical competence.

We examine both technical competence and a set of skills called information literacy. With the advent of the Internet, the ability to use technology requires not only technical acumen, but also the ability to search for and use information.

Information Literacy

Information literacy is the ability to recognize when information is needed and to locate, evaluate, and use effectively the needed information while adhering to principles of social responsibility.[6] Professional organizations associated with the American Library Association have defined information literacy standards for K–12 and for higher education. Although these standards were originally created with respect to students, they can easily be applied outside an academic setting and have special relevance for an individual's ability to use information sources on the web. An information-literate person would have the capacity to do the following:

- Determine the nature and the extent of the information needed
- Access needed information effectively and efficiently
- Evaluate information and its sources critically and incorporate selected information into his or her knowledge base and value system
- Use information effectively to accomplish a specific purpose
- Understand many of the economic, legal, and social issues surrounding the use of information, accessing and using information ethically and legally.[7]

Computer technology may be used for locating, evaluating, and using information, but a printed dictionary may also suit information needs. In fact, recognizing whether a printed or electronic source is more appropriate is one hallmark of an information-literate person. How is information literacy needed to use the web? Someone looking for information about a political issue might go to a common web search engine such as www.yahoo.com. Choosing key words for the search may require sufficient command of a topic to formulate the question using the correct terminology. Next, the user may be directed to consult an extensive list of directories. Choosing the appropriate directory is one more step to take. Reliability or bias of information is a common concern when consulting web resources, although it may be an issue in using print resources as well. With the fluidity of the web—the ease and low cost of widely disseminating information—these concerns are magnified. Sources may have been created by a scholarly research organization, a partisan group, or, as mentioned in *Next: The Future Just Happened,* by a very bright four-teen-year-old.[8]

There are very few works that address information literacy levels in the United States or in any country, for that matter.[9] One reason for this lack of research is the absence of measurement tools to assess information literacy, although some efforts are being made to develop the means to research this issue.[10] Of the few studies that exist, most of them are case studies that offer limited ability to assess the extent of information literacy in the population as a whole. One study conducted in a workplace setting in Australia, however, demonstrated that workers needed information literacy skills consisting of basic literacy (reading skills) and the ability to access information using technology, among other skills.[11]

Basic Literacy

Basic literacy is clearly a prerequisite for information literacy in the context of using resources on the web. Not surprisingly, one study of a technology center in a low-income community documented the problems that individuals with poor reading skills had in understanding content on the Internet.[12] Comprehensive and systematic data *are* available on literacy in the United States, and we can use this research to draw some inferences about information literacy needs. Funded by the U.S. Department of Education's National Center for Education Statistics, the National Adult Literacy Survey (NALS) was conducted in 1992.[13] A random sample of 26,000 American adults was interviewed. The survey defines three aspects of literacy: prose, document, and quantitative literacy. The first two categories pertain to the reading and comprehension skills traditionally associated with literacy, and the third is sometimes referred to as numeracy, or the ability to use and understand numbers. For the purposes of understanding information on the Internet, prose and document literacy are most relevant. Prose literacy calls for locating, integrating, and demonstrating comprehension of information in a variety of text forms, such as newspaper editorials, poems, fiction passages, or weather reports. Document literacy tasks include using forms or graphically displayed information "found in everyday life, including job applications, payroll forms, transportation schedules, maps, tables and graphs."[14] Literacy levels are scored separately for each type of literacy, and scores range from level 1 to level 5, with level 1 representing the lowest level of attainment.[15]

Results from the 1992 NALS are stunning. Approximately 21–23 percent of the adults in this country have skills at the lowest level of prose, document, and quantitative literacy.[16] Level 1 document literacy skills, for example, include the ability to complete a brief job application with just a few items or to sign on the correct line on a social security card. Prose literacy skills at this level consist of the ability to locate a single item in a short passage of text. An additional 25–28 percent were able to demonstrate skills at level 2, which required slightly more advanced, but still limited, reading and problem-solving abilities.[17] The lowest levels of attainment are of particular concern, because more than a fifth of the population was unable to perform simple daily tasks adequately. Limited fluency in English accounted for some, but certainly not all, of the results for the lowest categories of literacy.

What are the consequences for individuals with limited literacy, and for society? Although the results suggest startlingly low levels of literacy in the United States, participants were also asked whether they felt incapable of day-to-day functioning because of their literacy skills. For the most part, even those scoring at the lowest levels said they felt fairly comfortable coping with daily demands and expressed little need for assistance. The poor and near-poor have levels of literacy well below average, however, demonstrating a connection between literacy and earning ability.[18]

As the authors of the NALS study note, "If large percentages of adults had to do little more than be able to sign their name on a form or locate a single fact in a newspaper or table, then the levels of literacy seen in this survey might not warrant concern. We live in a nation, however, where both the volume and variety of written information are growing and where increasing numbers of citizens are expected to be able to read, understand, and use these materials."[19]

There are obvious parallels between the literacy definitions used by the NALS and the concept of information literacy. For example, the NALS was concerned with the ability of readers to process a number of categories or features, to decipher central information despite irrelevant distractors, and to cope with text that is lengthy and dense. These are prerequisites for understanding information on many Internet sites, which feature distractors such as advertisements or formats that are less than user-friendly. Beyond, this, however, Internet users need skills in searching for and evaluating information. Both of these require knowledge and experience, as a large body of research on information seeking shows.[20]

Although basic literacy appears to be most crucial to Internet use, its relationship to technology skills goes further. Anyone who has used technology of any sort knows that troubleshooting and problem solving are necessary at some point. Basic literacy is required to read manuals or online instructions. Being literate makes it possible to solve a problem or to learn the use of a more complicated device. Having noted the significance of basic literacy for technology use, we focus, however, on technical competence and information literacy.

Survey Results: Skills

In this section, we present data on skills needed to use computer technology from our national telephone survey. In order to assess the prevalence of both technical competence and information literacy, we asked a number of questions in our survey about the assistance individuals would need. The simple percentages, presented below, show ample need for assistance. More than half of the respondents reported some need for assistance with the most complex applications.

A substantial portion of our survey respondents reported needing assistance to carry out basic computer tasks. Nearly 22 percent said that they needed assistance using the mouse and keyboard—the most simple and yet fundamental skills involved in operating a computer. As tasks required more sophistication, the percentage of respondents needing help rose, with well over one-third needing assistance to find information on the web, find books, or do homework. One interesting finding was that the responses for our measures of information literacy were almost exactly the same, even though the questions were not asked consecutively.[21] For technical competence, there is a clear hierarchy of tasks. More than half the survey respondents require assistance to use common software applications such as word processing and spreadsheets. Looking at the simple percentages, we get a picture of a substantial minority that needs help taking the very first steps toward technical competence and larger segments of the popu-

WHAT MATTERS

Technical Competence

Do you need assistance doing the following computer tasks?

	Yes
Using the mouse and keyboard	22%
Using e-mail	31%
Using word processing/spreadsheet programs	52%

Information Literacy

Do you need assistance doing the following computer tasks?

	Yes
Finding books in a library	37%
Doing homework	37%
Finding information on the web	37%

lation needing help with more sophisticated applications, including those involving information literacy.

Using multivariate regression, we are able to find out which groups in the population are most likely to need help. We created an index for "technical competence," using the first three questions listed in the box above (assistance for using the mouse and keyboard, assistance for using e-mail, and assistance for using word processing and spreadsheet programs). We created a similar index for information literacy, using the responses for books, homework, and the Internet. The same explanatory variables used in the analysis of the access divide are included in our examination of data in this chapter, with one exception. We add the variable "library patronage," to find out whether individuals who use the library frequently are those who are most likely to need assistance. Other explanatory variables are gender, race, ethnicity, income, education, and age. The education variable is measured on a scale ranging from less than a high school degree to postgraduate study.[22]

The regression analyses reveal a skills divide that largely mirrors the access divide.[23] Individuals who are low-income, less-educated, older, and African American or Latino are more likely to need more computer assistance, controlling for other factors. This is true whether "skills" are defined as technical competence or information literacy. The results suggest that developing these skills is a complex process, involving access to computers, frequency of use, and also education or cognitive skills such as reading. Frequent library patrons, for example, are *less* likely to report needing assistance. Although there is no longer a gender divide in access, women are slightly more likely to report needing assistance for technical skills. In light of a prior gender gap in access, some women may have limited experience and less confidence about their technical skills. There are no gender differences for information literacy. All of these measures involve self-reported assessments of skills, of course, and therefore they are better viewed as perceived needs rather than objective assessments of the skills differences between groups.

We used Monte Carlo simulations to calculate the magnitude of skills differences—that is, the probability of needing computer assistance, holding other factors constant. Our hypothetical respondent is a white female who is a library patron with average education and income and of average age. We ran both the regression analyses and the simulations with the indices of technical competence and information literacy combined into a single index of skills, and also as separate indices. With the exception of gender, results were similar whether the indices were run separately or together. For the sake of simplicity, we present the results as a single index, except in the case of gender, where the results are for technical competence only.

While many factors influence skills, differences based on age and education are sharper than those based on other criteria. This is most noticeable for age, where there is an expected 32 percentage point difference between younger and older respondents. The predicted probability that a young individual, defined as age twenty-eight, will report needing assistance is only 20 percent, compared to an older individual, age sixty-one, who has a 52 percent probability of needing assistance (controlling for other factors). The predicted impact of education is somewhat less, 18 percentage points rather than 32. The expected probability that an individual with only a high school diploma will report needing assistance is 43 percent. For individuals with a college degree, the probability of needing assistance is 25 percent. Predicted differences for other factors were also significant, but more modest—a 12 percentage point difference between low- and high-income respondents, an 11 percentage point difference between

WHAT MATTERS

Who Is Most Likely to Need Assistance (technical competence and information literacy)?

Old (52% for 61-year-olds vs. 20% for 28-year-olds)—32-point difference

Less-educated (43% for high school diploma vs. 25% for bachelor's degree)—18-point difference

Poor (42% vs. 30% for affluent)—12-point difference

African Americans (45% vs. 34% for whites)—11-point difference

Latinos (42% vs. 34% for non-Latinos)—8-point difference

Who Is More Likely to Need Assistance for Technical Competence?

Females (34% vs. 33% for males)—1-point difference

No gender difference for information literacy

Note: Estimates are based on a hypothetical respondent who is female, white, and a library patron, with education, income, and age set at their means. The only statistically significant differences are the ones reported above (see tables A3.1 and A3.2). We have calculated the probability that respondents agree with the above statements, controlling for other factors.

African Americans and whites, and an 8 percentage point difference between Latinos and whites. For technical competence, the difference between men and women was statistically significant, but decidedly minor—only a little over 1 percentage point. Overall, then, skills differences largely duplicate disparities in access. This indicates that public policy enhancing both access and skills development would be effective if targeted to low-income communities in particular, where many residents also have lower levels of education.

Public Policy Addressing Skills: Libraries and Community Technology Centers

Despite the absence of data on technical competence and information literacy skills in the United States, some programs are intended to promote skills as well as access. Both government and nonprofit efforts have focused on two venues for skills development among adults—public libraries and community technology centers (CTCs). CTCs may be located in a multiservice agency, a stand-alone computing center, housing development, church, library, or other places in low-income urban and rural communities. There are approximately 400 federally funded CTCs across the country, and some centers are supported by nonprofit organizations as well as grants from private foundations.[24]

Libraries provide the most extensive network for public access and are an important source of computer assistance. Almost half of the public libraries in the United States now offer some type of computer training, either in technical skills or in the skills needed to evaluate information on the web.[25] We know little, however, about the extent of the training offered, its quality, its availability in poor communities, or whether the supply of training satisfies the demand. Both the public and the library profession strongly support the technological function of libraries.

The role of the public library as "safety net" for information have-nots is an important one in the eyes of many library leaders and library users. A Benton Foundation report, based on a public opinion poll and interviews with library leaders, provided a sense of the place the public library has now and in the future in American culture. Some of the roles of the public library include providing a physical place for a community to gather, "the library as a provider and protector of equal access and equal opportunity; [and] the library as community builder, civic integrator, and community activist in a digital world."[26]

In the foundation's national public opinion poll of 1,015 adults, respondents indicated a strong public support of the library as a provider of access. For example, 85 percent of the respondents believed that it is either very important (60 percent) or moderately important (25 percent) for a public library to spend its money "providing computers and online services to children and adults who don't have their own computers."[27] Similarly, 86 percent of the respondents thought the library should spend its money "providing a place where librarians help people find information through computers and online services."[28]

A few studies have examined the activities and impact of CTCs. One survey of 123 CTC administrators found that access to technology and the Internet were the most important functions of CTCs but that literacy classes and tutoring were also provided at some centers.[29] The CTCNet Research and Evaluation Team conducted a survey of 817 people at forty-four CTC affiliates in 1998. Findings from this study indicate that activities in CTCs include the development of English-language skills, homework, GED (general education development, for high school equivalency) courses, use of e-mail, Internet searches, and the creation of webpages. Reasons for taking classes at a CTC were dominated by job-related needs. For example, "65 percent of respondents took classes at a technology center to improve their job skills [and] 30 percent used the Internet at their center to look for a job."[30] More than a third of the respondents felt they had improved their job skills or had success in finding a job as a result of programs at the CTC. Participants also felt more positive about their ability to learn new skills or pursue further education. More than half of the respondents rated "finding out about local events, local government, or state/federal government as important reasons for coming to their center" (ctcnet.org/impact98.htm).[31] Some of these CTC users— about 23 percent—used computers in their own homes but apparently went to the CTC for training. The top reason for attending a CTC was its "comfortable, supportive atmosphere," and 94 percent of the CTC users who participated in the study were overwhelmingly supportive of the CTC and its programs.

This federally sponsored evaluation is interesting for the picture it paints of activities within CTCs, but it is important to note that many areas lack such facilities. Community-based programs are often small and frequently rely upon unstable funding sources and part-time or volunteer staff. A Los Angeles–area study conducted by the Tomas Rivera Policy Institute at Claremont College found that, in many poor neighborhoods, the public library offered the only available public access.[32]

The sparse evidence on CTC and library technology programs affords little guidance for policy. Does it matter where access and skills programs are available—would more people attend them at libraries or at other places in the community? Do disadvantaged groups view libraries, where the majority of programs are located now, in a negative light? Help with computer skills can take several forms, from personal instruction to manuals. We also wondered whether any of these methods were preferred over others and whether the choices made by disadvantaged groups differed from the population as a whole.

Survey Results: Preferences for Public Access and Learning

As part of our survey, we asked questions about willingness to use different locations for public access, and as reported in the next section, about preferences for learning new skills.

Public Access Sites

The majority of respondents were willing to go to a number of places to use computers and the Internet: recreation centers (64 percent), senior centers (60 percent), churches (66 percent), and government offices (59 percent). The most popular sites, however, were schools (74 percent) and public libraries (93 percent). Schools and libraries are public institutions that bear responsibility for education and that could be expected to offer assistance and expertise. They have also been a focus of government programs to increase the number of computers in low-income communities, although not all school computer facilities are open after hours or available for the use of nonstudents.

Do any disadvantaged groups differ from the general population in their willingness to use public access sites? Six questions from our survey measure willingness to use computers and the Internet in different public places—recreation centers, senior centers, local churches, government offices, libraries, and public schools after hours. We combined these questions to create an index ranging from 0 to 6 of reported willingness to use public access. The index serves as the dependent variable in our statistical model. The explanatory factors included in the model are the social and demographic variables used in the multivariate regression model for the access divide.

We found that the individuals who expressed the most willingness to use public access sites were more affluent, better educated, and African American.[33] Controlling for income and education, African Americans are *more* likely than whites to express interest in using a range of public access sites. Asians were less likely than other racial groups to express willingness to use public access. Unfortunately, however, the low-income and less-educated individuals for whom public access is intended are least likely to be willing to use public access sites. And, we know from our question about the places where people *actually use* computers, that only about 13 percent of those who have no home computer use library computers, in contrast to 15 percent of those who do have home computers.

Libraries are already cornerstones of public access policy and were the most preferred setting for public access. Are there ways in which use of the library could be expanded or improved, particularly for disadvantaged groups? Perhaps. According to our survey, they are among the groups in the population who are most likely to think of libraries as "community gathering places." Only slightly more than half (51 percent) of respondents viewed libraries as community gathering places, yet low-income individuals, women, African Americans, and Latinos were most likely to see libraries in this manner, controlling for library patronage and other factors.[34] This image may be one that libraries should capitalize on in poor and minority communities, particularly in efforts to expand technology access. The CTC evaluations indicate that sociability and a "comfortable, supportive" atmosphere

---

WHAT MATTERS

Who Is Most Willing to Use Public Access?
Affluent
Educated
African Americans
(Asian Americans were less willing than whites to use public access.)

Who Sees Libraries as "Community Gathering Places"?
Poor
Women
Latinos
African Americans

Note: The only statistically significant differences are the ones reported above (table A3.3). When multivariate regression is used, these are the variables that matter, holding other factors constant.

were critical reasons for using the facilities, and this is likely important in providing assistance in other venues, such as libraries.

Instructional Preferences

We also asked our respondents how they felt about various methods of providing assistance—one-on-one help, group instruction, online help, and printed manuals. We wondered whether any particular method of instruction was preferred in general, or by specific groups, and whether any particular method posed obstacles for learning for specific groups. Such information could be used to improve assistance provided in libraries, CTCs, and other settings. Although many people were willing to use any form of assistance, negative reactions rose as instruction became less personal and hands-on. A majority of respondents was willing to use any method of assistance, but a sizeable minority expressed discomfort with less personal methods, particularly those that require more reading and self-help. Support for online instruction and printed manuals was weakest (about two-thirds) and support for one-on-one instruction was highest (89 percent). The simple percentages for instructional preferences are reported in the box below.

To explore the differences between groups, we used multivariate regression to analyze responses to each of the four types of instruc-

WHAT MATTERS

Instructional Preferences

Would you be willing to learn a new skill through . . .

One-on-one instruction	89% agree; 6% disagree
Group instruction (such as a class)	78% agree; 16% disagree
Online help or tutorials	64% agree; 22% disagree
Printed manuals	67% agree; 23% disagree

Note: We have combined the "strongly agree" and "agree" responses and the "strongly disagree" and "disagree" into the categories agree and disagree. The percentages total less than 100% because we have omitted missing responses as well as those recorded as "neutral" or "don't know."

tion. The explanatory variables used for each question were the demographic variables used for the access divide, and library patronage was used as a control.[35]

For instructional preferences, we found that certain groups were more likely to be reticent about some methods of assistance. Women were more likely than men to prefer one-on-one instruction, whereas men liked do-it-yourself methods such as online instruction and tutorials. Income mattered for only one category, with poor people more hesitant than affluent respondents about using computer-based help such as online instruction and tutorials. Older individuals and

WHAT MATTERS

Who Is Most Likely to Prefer Learning New Skills in This Way?

One-on-One Instruction
Educated
Young
Women

Group Instruction
Educated
Young
Latinos
African Americans (Asian Americans are less likely to prefer group instruction than whites.)

Online Instruction or Tutorials
Affluent
Educated
Young
Men
African Americans

Printed Manuals
Young
African Americans

Note: The only statistically significant differences are the ones reported above (see table A3.4). When multivariate regression is used, these are the variables that matter, holding other factors constant.

less-educated individuals are more inclined toward rejecting most or all methods of instruction. This may indicate a general anxiety about computer instruction or a lack of interest in learning computer skills.

Some interesting patterns emerged with regard to race and ethnicity. Controlling for other factors, African Americans have even *more positive* attitudes about learning computer skills than the general population. African Americans were similar to whites in terms of personal instruction and were less likely than whites to oppose other methods. Both Latinos and African Americans were less likely than whites to oppose group instruction or computer classes. Asian Americans, however, were less likely than whites to be willing to participate in group instruction. Overall, this suggests that a range of approaches is needed, particularly for men and women. Education and age clearly affect general willingness to receive instruction. Racial and ethnic groups reporting lower skills—African Americans and Latinos—are not particularly opposed to any method of instruction, compared with whites. African Americans, in fact, are *less* likely than whites to express opposition to several types of instruction.

Conclusion

This chapter serves as further argument that an information technology gap indeed exists and is characterized by a skills divide as well as an access divide. The two are not entirely separable in practice, of course, but the implications of a skills divide lie at the heart of the policy problem—do individuals have the skills they need to participate fully in society, particularly in the economic and political arenas? Without appropriate skills, access is meaningless. Information technology requires a set of computer-specific skills that we call technical competencies, but many uses of the Internet also demand more general information literacy, rooted in basic literacy. The proliferation of websites offering information on health, jobs, parenting, political issues and campaigns, homework topics, home remodeling, cooking, money management, and an unfathomable number of subjects requires the ability to locate, read, comprehend, and evaluate information (both its content and its source).

Our findings on skills show a sizeable minority bereft of the most basic technical abilities. About one-fifth of the population reported needing assistance using a mouse or a keyboard. Likewise, more than one-third of respondents felt they needed help in negotiating their way through information sources on the web and in databases. Public provision of access accompanied by on-site assistance offers opportunities to teach basic skills, to provide more sophisticated technical support, to instruct individuals in using search engines and evaluating sources, and to help with specific information searches. Some libraries and CTCs are already providing library Internet service, though we know little about the extent or quality of the help that is offered in most of these settings.

Large majorities of individuals expressed willingness to use computers and the Internet at public access sites, and the majority of respondents showed flexibility in expressing willingness to use multiple methods for learning new skills or coping with computer problems. Respondents were most amenable to personal instruction and classes and slightly less favorable toward self-help in the form of online instruction, tutorials, or manuals. More sobering, though, is the reality revealed in the prior chapter, which showed that only about 10–15 percent of the population uses technology resources at libraries, which are the most common site for public access. People without home access are slightly less likely to use such services. Apparently, the willingness reported in our survey is seldom translated into deed.

By disaggregating this data, we get a better picture of who lacks skills and the preferences that these same groups have regarding public access and assistance. For the most part, the skills divide replicates the access divide—those who lack skills are older, less-educated, poor, African American, and Latino. The same pattern of disparity characterizes both technical competence and information literacy. Although there was a small gender difference in technical competence, controlling for other factors, it was too small to raise much concern about a skills gap affecting women.

Confirmation of a skills divide that parallels the access divide presents a policy challenge. Even if computers are becoming increasingly affordable, some individuals may face significant hurdles in using them, particularly if those left behind are the least educated with the fewest resources for learning through trial-and-error and through the manuals and tutorials provided by manufacturers. The web offers new opportunities for enriching people's lives in many ways, but it also poses more skill demands than simple computer tasks. The policy challenge is how to offer assistance to those who lack skills, at least to those who are interested. The poor and the least educated are *less* willing to use public access sites, where assistance could be provided. Older and low-income individuals are also less willing to learn new skills, in whatever form. These findings, however, need to be placed in the context of the favorable attitudes that most people had about public access and instruction. Those who are poor, older, and less-educated are somewhat less positive.

Race and ethnicity influence preferences for addressing the skills divide, but the news here is hopeful rather than disheartening. African Americans were more willing to use public access and more positive about various methods of assistance than white respondents. Latinos expressed slightly more positive attitudes toward libraries as community gathering places than non-Latinos, but were equally willing to use public access. Latinos preferred group instruction to a greater extent than whites did but differed little in other respects. Although Asian Americans were more likely to reject public access and group classes, they enjoy higher rates of home access than did whites and are not disadvantaged in terms of skills.

On a final note, gender made a difference in learning preferences. Men were more likely to want to find their own way with online help and tutorials, while women tended to choose personal instruction. This suggests that personal assistance and public access may be more important for women or used as occasional technical support by men.

Having established the outlines of the access and skills divides, we turn next toward their implications for daily life—for earning a living and exercising the rights and responsibilities of democratic citizenship.

Notes

1. Pearson and Young 2002, 3.

2. See Pearson and Young 2002, 3. The National Academy of Sciences provides a three-part framework for technological literacy that includes knowledge, ways of thinking and acting, and capabilities that apply to any type of technology, not just information technology (1996, 4). The International Technology Education Association (ITEA) has defined standards for technological literacy in K–12 education (International Technology Educa-

tion Association 2002). There are twenty different standards, including knowledge of historical and cultural attributes of technology, engineering design, and transportation, manufacturing, and construction technologies.

3. Horrigan 2002. The survey was conducted by Pew researchers in 2001.

4. U.S. Department of Commerce 2002.

5. Horrigan and Rainie 2002.

6. American Library Association 1989.

7. In 2000, the Association of College and Research Libraries, a division of the American Library Association, created *Information Literacy Competency Standards for Higher Education*, upon which the above definition is based. Similar competencies have been defined for the K–12, as well as adult, populations. The K–12 population is addressed by the American Association of School Librarians (1998) in *Information Power: Building Partnerships for Student Learning* with its information literacy standards for student learning.

8. Lewis 2001.

9. The absence of data applies for information literacy in the K–12 setting, higher education, or adults in the workplace. The information literacy movement was born in school library media centers, and there is an extensive body of publication on the topic. These publications, however, tend to be either tool kits and worksheets for teaching information literacy skills or professional editorials and opinion pieces about the necessity of teaching information literacy skills. There are some case studies and anecdotal reports of information literacy programs, but there is no body of data.

10. A promising project undertaken by Kent State University Libraries and Media Services faculty is the development of a measurement tool for higher education. This tool, tentatively titled Standard Assessment of Information Literacy Skills (SAILS), is being considered for broad use by member institutions of the Association of College and Research Libraries. If this tool is adopted and widely applied, data can be collected and analyzed for establishing norms of information literacy skills. Until that adoption occurs, though, there is no source of data for describing the level of information literacy skills.

11. McMahon and Bruce (2002) published a study of information literacy needs. Their phenomenographic approach was intended to derive a better understanding of the perception of information literacy needs among staff participating in community development projects in Australia. Using interviews with five development workers, McMahon and Bruce constructed a

multilayered model of necessary information literacy skills for one particular work setting. Their model, which is based on the perceptions of the workers, began with basic literacy. From basic literacy outward, the model incorporated workplace system skills, information technology skills, cultural experiences, ability to translate between cultures, information presentation, and relevance to the community being served. A broadening of the initial model accommodates five layers of information literacy: (1) basic literacy skills, (2) understanding workplace systems, (3) communication skills, (4) accessing information sources, and (5) understanding the dominant society.

12. Penuel and Kim 2000.

13. Another survey is scheduled for 2002.

14. Kaestle et al. 2001.

15. Ibid.

16. The range of percentages reported reflects estimates for the whole population based on the sample of 26,000 participants.

17. Level 3 was achieved by about 61 million adults, which constitutes nearly one-third of participants. Levels 4 and 5 were attained by 18–21 percent of the participants, with only 3 percent of adults performing at the highest level.

18. National Center for Education Statistics [no date].

19. Kirsch et al. 2002, xxi. For a complete description of the definitions, questions and tasks used in the survey, and the results of the 1992 study, consult Kaestle et al. 2001.

20. The vast body of information-seeking research is primarily out of the disciplines of library science, information science, communication science, cognitive psychology, cognitive science, human-computer interaction, and education.

21. Percentages are rounded. There was some minor variation in the frequency of responses for the three questions.

22. Library usage was measured on a five-point Likert scale based on the number of times the respondent reported going to the library in the last month: 0 times, 1–5 times, 6–10 times, 11–15 times, and more than 15 times. Dummy variables were created for gender, race, ethnicity, and income. Women, African Americans, Latinos, Asian Americans, and those with annual incomes less than $30,000 were coded 1; otherwise, respondents were coded 0. For race/ethnicity, non-Latino whites are the reference, or left-out, group. Education was measured on a five-point Likert scale, with responses coded 1 for less than a high school degree and ranging to 5 for postgraduate work. Age was recorded in years.

23. See tables A2.1 and A2.2 for the results of the ordered logistic regression analysis.

24. For a description of the CTC program, see U.S. Department of Education 2002.

25. Trotter 2001.

26. Benton Foundation 1996, 11. The report was funded by the W. K. Kellogg Foundation.

27. Ibid., 44.

28. Ibid., 44.

29. Servon and Nelson 2001, 285–86.

30. Chow et al. 1998.

31. Ibid.

32. Trotter 2001.

33. For the results of the ordered logistic regression analysis, see table A3.3.

34. These results are based on logistic regression reported in table A3.3, using a binary dependent variable (agree or disagree that the library is a community gathering place). The independent variables used in the multivariate model were income, education, age, gender, Latino, African American, and Asian American, as measured in the access chapter, with the addition of library patronage as a control variable. Library patronage was measured on an ordinal scale as the number of times the respondent had visited the library in the past month.

35. The results of the multivariate regression analysis are reported in table A3.4 We used negative responses for coding the dependent variable, although, for clarity, we present the results in the positive. (For example, where poor individuals were less likely to favor a certain method of instruction, we show that affluent individuals prefer that method.) Since the majority of respondents supported any single type of instruction, we were most interested in whether certain groups of respondents were likely to shun any particular method.

Chapter 4

The Economic Opportunity Divide

A consensus has emerged among observers in academia, government, and business that there is indeed something new about the economy and that technological change is one of the factors underlying this transformation. On the left, Manuel Castells has characterized the present period of capitalist development as "informationalism." On the right, William Niskanen, conservative economist and director of the Heritage Foundation, calls the current era the "third industrial revolution," ushered in by digital technology and biotechnology. The U.S. Department of Commerce has dropped the term "emerging" from its reports on the "digital economy." And the Conference Board, a business organization whose economic reports are closely watched by policymakers and industry, has compared information technology to "steam power at the turn of the nineteenth century and electricity at the beginning of the twentieth."[1]

What skills do workers need to survive, and perhaps even prosper, in this new economy? Are information-technology skills linked to economic opportunity; if so, how are they related? Does an "economic opportunity divide," based on lack of computer skills, exist? The first section of this chapter traces the trajectory of economic change over the past few decades. A broad economic restructuring has widened economic disparities, automated some jobs out of existence, created new types of jobs, modified organizational practices, and altered traditional career ladders. In the "new economy," workers are more likely to hold a number of jobs over a lifetime. Less-educated workers have watched their standard of living erode, and skills demands are increasing even in jobs requiring only a high school degree or less. We contend that computer skills must be viewed as one element of changing skills requirements in the new economy and that they are particularly important for mobility beyond the lowest-paying jobs.

Against this backdrop of economic change, we discuss our data on the attitudes and experiences of our respondents in regard to computers and economic opportunity. Technology has the potential to enhance economic opportunity in three distinct ways: for use on the job, for finding a job, and for learning. First, technology skills can facilitate employment or advancement in jobs or business. Second, the Internet offers tools for searching for a job and for gathering information about occupations and their requirements. Third, computer software and the Internet provide users with choices for improving other basic skills or earning educational or occupational credentials. Lifelong learning promises to be an important consideration for economic advancement now and in the foreseeable future.

We ask respondents about their attitudes regarding computer skills and economic opportunity in all three of these areas, as well as their experiences in using technology for job searches and online courses. Our low-income sample allows us to explore the perceptions and possible motivations of those who are most likely to lack computer skills. Do disadvantaged groups see information technology as less important for economic opportunity than do other Americans? Are they indifferent to its potential for economic advancement? What are the characteristics of those who have used new technologies for job search and learning, and how interested are disadvantaged groups and other Americans in using the Internet for these purposes? Some major studies have tracked the way in which Americans are using the Internet, but none of these previous studies examine the attitudes of both users and nonusers.[2] Understanding the priorities and aspirations of nonusers or those with limited skills suggests future directions for public policy.

The beliefs expressed by survey respondents demonstrate that the problem lies not with limited awareness of technology's benefits, but with issues of access and skill. An economic opportunity divide does in fact exist, but some disadvantaged groups see technology in a particularly positive light, and those attitudes may help to eventually bridge the divide.

Economic Opportunity in the "New Economy"

Rapid growth in the productivity of the U.S. economy in the late 1990s resulted primarily from a groundswell in information technology use across a wide range of industries rather than from growth in firms that produce hardware or software.[3] Despite the demise of the dot.com mania, technology has enabled broader innovations in production processes and products that will continue to affect the economy. According to the international Organization for Economic Cooperation and Development, innovations made possible by information technology "are transforming the ways in which economies, and the people within them, are working."[4] Among these dramatic shifts are rising skills requirements in the labor force and changes in the opportunity structure for American workers.

Education and Economic Opportunity

Educational attainment is increasingly linked to both economic opportunity and widening disparities in the labor market. Controlling for race, experience, and other factors, male college graduates averaged 42 percent more in earnings than male high school graduates in 1999. This college "premium" has more than doubled since 1979, when male college graduates earned an average of 20 percent more than did male high school graduates.[5] The expanding wage differential is partly due to gains made by college-educated workers, who experienced real growth in wages over this period. It also reflects deteriorating earnings for every category of educational attainment below a bachelor's degree, particularly those with only a high school education or less.[6]

Income inequality has been growing in the United States for more than two decades now, and it was only during the rapid growth and tight labor market of the late 1990s that this trend abated somewhat.[7] Two divergent tendencies characterized the 1980s and early 1990s: rising incomes at the top of the income distribution and falling real wages for many at the middle and bottom. The number of full-time, year-round workers whose earnings fall below the poverty line has been climbing since 1973, even when the figures are adjusted for changes in the size of the workforce over this period.[8] During the latter half of the 1990s, the flush economy began to improve the situation of the poorest Americans, narrowing the gap between the bottom and middle of the wage distribution. Nevertheless, these changes were insufficient to reverse the trends of the past few decades—inequality today is still worse than in previous periods of economic expansion, such as the 1960s. Because improvements for the lowest-paid workers were due primarily to low unemployment, the economy's subsequent slide has jeopardized the gains realized at the close of the 1990s.[9] Recent reports indicate that the both the proportion of Americans living in poverty and income inequality sharply increased during 2001.[10]

Women and racial and ethnic minorities continue to lag far behind white men in earnings, despite gaining some ground over the past few decades. For racial and ethnic minorities, some, but not all of the differences are attributable to median age and education. Fewer African Americans and Latinos of working age have bachelor's degrees than whites—only one-fifth of African Americans and one-seventh of Latinos, compared to one-third of whites.[11]

Education affects the ability of workers to chart a course through an increasingly volatile labor market. Steady employment and upward mobility are more difficult for less-educated workers. Blue collar workers are most likely to be displaced through layoffs, although during the 1990s white collar workers suffered from downsizing more frequently than in previous decades. Women, nonwhites, and workers lacking college degrees are the slowest to find new employment after a job loss.[12] Approximately 11 percent of the workforce is persistently "stuck" in low-wage jobs for five years or more. Most frequently, these workers lack more than a high school education and work in jobs that offer the least in the way of training and advancement. Even some postsecondary education makes income mobility more likely.[13] One study of career mobility and lifetime earnings found that the penalty for lack of education experienced by workers with a high school diploma or less actually grew with years of work experience.[14]

The growing returns to education are driven in part by technological change and the demand for higher levels of skill in the workforce. Education is clearly an important dimension of opportunity in the new economy. How do computer skills affect the fortunes of American workers, especially those who are in nonprofessional jobs?

Looking at the Numbers:
Computers and the Workplace

Information technology has wrought a number of changes in the workplace and continues to grow rapidly by several measures. The U.S. Bureau of Labor Statistics, for example, projects that the fastest-growing occupations through the year 2010 will include software engineers, computer support specialists, network and systems administrators, database administrators, systems analysts, and desktop publishers. In fact, of the ten fastest-growing occupations, eight are computer-related.

Technology makes its real impact felt, however, through its integration in a variety of workplace tasks. Office work has been revolutionized by word processing, spreadsheets, and databases. Advanced manufacturing technology uses computers to control production processes and to diversify and customize products. The trucking industry now uses software for planning routes, controlling costs, scheduling, and real-time tracking.[15] Computers have also made possible new practices such as "just-in-time" inventory, and this potential has been expanded by the development of the Internet and e-commerce.

The diffusion of information technology throughout U.S. industry is at an early stage, according to some observers. Digital technology promises to be adopted in a broader range of applications in the future.[16] Data on the use of the Internet support this contention. In the span of just thirteen months, between August 2000 and September 2001, the percentage of employed adults twenty-five years of age and older who use the Internet and/or e-mail at work rose from 26 percent to nearly 42 percent. This suggests that newer applications, especially those using the Internet, are proliferating in the workplace.[17]

Computers and Less-Educated Workers

What these general data do not tell us, however, is what the accelerating diffusion of computer applications means for job applicants and current workers who are stuck on the wrong side of the access and skills divides. Jobs that require a high school diploma or less are commonly referred to as "low-skill" jobs.[18] How, then, do computer skills affect the chances that workers have for obtaining these low-skill jobs and for possibly advancing to moderately-skilled jobs that require some postsecondary education, such as an associate's degree, an apprenticeship, or vocational training?

Nearly half of the workers in low-skill jobs currently use computers in some way at work, according to our survey and other data collected over the past few years.[19] Forty-eight percent of our respondents who were employed and had a high school education or less used the computer at work at least once during the month prior to our survey. This was substantially lower than the 65 percent of all employed persons who reported using computers at work, but it still represents a near majority of noncollege workers. A smaller share of noncollege workers reported intensive use of information technology on the job—17 percent used the computer frequently (between 31 and 100 times) at work during the past month, and 10 percent used it very frequently (more than 100 times). Our data, based on the reports of individual workers, are consistent with employer surveys, which show that 50 to 60 percent of jobs requiring a high school education or less involve some computer use. Our data strengthen the case that computer use is significant in these types of jobs, because they are based on reports of actual use rather than reported employer requirements.

One of the problems with tracking only "computer use" is that individuals and employers may be reporting simple applications, such as optical scanning, that do not involve any of the skills discussed in the last chapter. A more challenging threshold for measuring computer use, however, is Internet use on the job. The results of our own survey reveal that a sizeable minority of employed workers with a high school education or less—25 percent—used the Internet at work during the past month. This is significantly lower than the 45 percent of all employed workers who reported using the Internet at work, but clearly even less-educated workers are using relatively demanding forms of digital technology.

Our survey data and other reports establish that computer use is prevalent in the workplace. Computer use rises with educational level, but even among those with only a high school diploma or less, nearly half of those who work reported using a computer at work, and one-quarter used the Internet. The recent surge of Internet use in the workplace demonstrates that job requirements for technology use are important and may become more widespread in the near future.

Are workers who lack any type of computer skill essentially shut out of the job market? The answer is clearly no, based on our survey findings as well as employer surveys.[20] Despite the increased use of technology in the workplace, jobs requiring little computer use or very simple computer use are among those projected to have the largest growth (in terms of the actual number of jobs rather than the rate of growth). These include fast food workers, retail salespersons, cashiers, security guards, and waiters and waitresses.[21] The problem, then, is not so much a matter of access to any employment. A number of low-skill, low-wage jobs with limited upward mobility will continue to be available to workers lacking even the most rudimentary computer skills.

Workers with no computer skills, however, may be less able to move into jobs that offer better pay and benefits. Whereas service workers, factory workers, and laborers have the lowest rate of computer use in the workforce, the demand for computer use is higher in occupations requiring more skill or experience, such as skilled trades or technical, sales, and administrative support.[22] To examine the relationship between computers and economic opportunity, however, we need to look more closely at the issue of skills.

Rising Skill Requirements

Computer use is proliferating, but computer skills alone are not enough to open the door to economic opportunity. There is a consensus among researchers that skills requirements are rising, even in jobs requiring a high school degree or less.[23] Computer skills are often cited as the most common change in job requirements.[24] But other basic skills, such as reading or math, and "soft skills," or interpersonal skills such as dealing with customers, are often at least as important to employers.[25] As the chapter on the skills divide demonstrates, technical competence is necessary but not sufficient to use the Internet. Likewise, technical competence should be viewed as just one part of a package of skills that are increasingly in demand.

Technological change has helped raise skills requirements. Adapting to new technologies requires basic literacy and numeracy—to read and write instructions, study new training materials, and perform simple math. Computers have facilitated the adoption of participatory "high-performance" workplace practices, such as total quality management, which requires statistical control of production processes. These organizational practices tend to upgrade necessary skill levels for front-line workers.[26] Some jobs have also experienced an "upskilling" effect, where workers assume new, more demanding responsibilities with the assistance of information technology. In the insurance industry, for example, clerical workers using desktop PCs now perform underwriting as well as basic data entry.[27] The requisite skills may include learning new software programs, but demands for problem-solving, literacy, and numeracy are at least as critical.

A widely cited government report released in the early 1990s made the case that improving a broad range of skills throughout the workforce was critical for competition in a global economy. The Secretary's Commission on Achieving Necessary Skills (SCANS) defined a number of core workforce competencies for the new economy, on the basis of research and consultation with employers. The SCANS requirement for information competence is similar to technical competency and information literacy as defined in the previous chapter. Workers meeting these standards "can acquire and evaluate data, organize and maintain files, interpret and communicate, and use computers to process information."[28] Such competencies, however, rely upon foundation skills such as reading, writing, and arithmetic.

Computer and cognitive skills may be more valued in jobs that offer better pay and benefits for less-educated workers. One study found that jobs requiring only soft skills were often part time, with no benefits and median pay just above the minimum wage.[29] Another study found that companies in rural areas that required computer, reading, writing, and math skills were often larger firms that paid their employees more.[30]

Computer skills are best viewed as part of a package of basic skills, along with literacy and numeracy, which can enhance an individual's employability for a broader range of occupations. Moreover, technological competence and information literacy can be valuable when searching for better jobs or for learning. Computers can help workers hone basic skills, take advantage of job-specific training opportunities, and further their education.

Attitudes about Computer Skills
and Economic Opportunity

What do we know based on the survey, about beliefs regarding information technology and opportunity? Are those who are less likely to
have access and skills also less interested in technology? In particular,
are they less likely to be motivated by the prospect of economic
returns for computer skills? The attitudes expressed by respondents
reveal the relative value that different groups, especially those from
low-income communities, place on the connection between technology and opportunity.

A solid majority of all respondents—more than two-thirds—artic-
ulated the belief that computer skills are linked to economic opportunity in a variety of ways. Of the 1,837 valid responses to the survey, 69
percent agreed with the general statement that it is "necessary for people to use the Internet to keep up with the times." Similar majorities
also agreed that learning new computer skills was important for career
advancement. When asked, "Do you believe you need to learn new
computer skills to get a job?" 70 percent said yes. Similarly, 71 percent
thought learning new computer skills was important for securing a
higher-paying job, and three-quarters of respondents believed learning
new computer skills was necessary for starting a small business. A lower
percentage of respondents—61 percent—felt that learning new computer skills was necessary to obtain a promotion.

What do these findings tell us? The similarity between responses
for the general statement about "keeping up with the times" and the
responses to the various measures of economic advancement—getting a job, getting a promotion, getting a higher-paying job, and starting a small business—indicates that these individuals are expressing
general beliefs about technology and opportunity as well as commenting on their own specific skills or needs. For example, although
the vast majority of respondents—70 percent—agreed with the statement "You need to learn new computer skills to get a job," only 6.5
percent reported having been denied a job because they needed more
computer skills.

What factors account for variation in beliefs about the connection
between computer skills and economic opportunity? Using multivariate regression, we compared the results of two models. In the first
one, the dependent variable, or the result to be explained, is the state-

ment that it is necessary for people to use the Internet to keep up with the times. Positive responses were coded 1, and negative responses were coded 0.[31] For the second model, the dependent variable is an index of responses to the following four questions measuring beliefs about the significance of computer skills and economic opportunity: (1) Do you believe you need to learn new computer skills to get a job? (2) Do you believe you need to learn new computer skills to get a higher-paying job? (3) Do you believe you need to learn new computer skills to get a promotion? (4) Do you believe you need to learn new computer skills to start a small business?[32] For both models, higher scores are associated with more favorable attitudes toward the use of computer skills for economic opportunity.

The same explanatory variables used in the analysis of the access divide are included in our examination of data in this chapter, with one exception. We add the variable *employment status* so that we can take into account whether respondents are employed. Other explanatory variables are gender, race, ethnicity, income, education, and age. The education variable is measured on a scale ranging from less than a high school degree to postgraduate study.

WHAT MATTERS

Who Is Most Likely to Think You Need the Internet to Keep Up?

Latinos (80% vs. 65% for whites)—15-point difference

African Americans (78% vs. 65% for whites)—13-point difference

Who Thinks You Need More Computer Skills to Get Ahead?

Young (73% for 28-year-olds vs. 55% for 61-year-olds)—18-point difference

African Americans (76% vs. 66% for whites)—10-point difference

Unemployed (74% vs. 67% for employed)—7-point difference

Females (67% vs. 63% for males)—4-point difference

Note: Estimates are based on a hypothetical respondent who is female, white, and employed, with values for education, age, and income set at their mean for the sample. The only statistically significant differences are the ones reported above (see table A4.1). We have calculated the probability that respondents agree with the above statements, controlling for other factors.

Our analysis indicates that race and ethnicity are particularly important for predicting attitudes regarding information technology and economic advancement. When we asked a general question about technology use that was unrelated to the respondent's beliefs about his or her own skills, attitudes did not differ by age, education, or income. Racial differences were the only statistically significant predictors of beliefs about the Internet. After we controlled for socioeconomic conditions, gender, age, and employment status, African Americans and Latinos were statistically more likely than whites to believe that it is necessary to use the Internet to keep up with the times. On the basis of the multivariate analysis, we estimate the probability of agreeing that the Internet is necessary to keep up with the times as 80 percent for Latinos, 78 percent for African Americans, and 65 percent for whites. The paradox is that Latinos and African Americans have significantly lower access to the Internet and report the need for more assistance in using it.

Similarly, African Americans (but not Latinos) were significantly more likely than whites to view the acquisition of new computer skills as a means of career advancement—for starting a business or for obtaining a job, a higher-paying job, or a promotion. There was a 76 percent probability of African American respondents agreeing that they needed to learn new skills for economic advancement versus a 66 percent probability of a similar response from whites.

Women, the young, and the unemployed were statistically more likely to cite the necessity of learning new computer skills, although they were not more likely to believe that using the Internet was necessary to keep up with the times. Women were slightly more likely to state that new skills were necessary for economic advancement—with a 67 percent probability of agreement with the statement, compared with a 63 percent probability for men. The unemployed were also more likely to agree with the statement "You need to learn new computer skills" for economic advancement. For the unemployed, the probability of agreeing with this statement is 74 percent, versus 67 percent for employed respondents. In light of the fact that African Americans are among the likely groups to report needing assistance with computers, these responses may reflect some feelings about their own personal skills as well as general beliefs about the significance of these skills for economic opportunity.

The greatest differences in attitudes are based on age. The probability that young respondents agreed with the statements in the index was 72 percent versus 66 percent for middle-aged respondents and 55 percent for older respondents. For the young (age twenty-eight), who are more likely to have both access and skills, agreement with the statement reflects generally positive attitudes about the significance of technology. Older individuals have possibly reached a point in their careers at which they are less concerned with advancement and learning new skills, even if they have not yet retired. Older respondents may also be more apathetic in general about technology use.

Surprisingly, attitudes about computer skills—using the Internet to keep up with the times and the linkage between computers and economic advancement—did not vary by income or education. Low-income and less-educated individuals, therefore, are just as likely as other Americans to value the potential connection between technology skills and economic opportunity. This reflects a broad consensus on these issues and suggests that, for most groups (other than older individuals), the access and skills divides are not usually the result of indifference to information technology and its potential.

Economic Opportunity and Information Networks

Labor force projections depict a future in which workers of all skill levels will change jobs several times over the course of their careers.[33] Computers and the Internet offer information for job search and networking that can be advantageous to less-educated workers. Our survey findings explore attitudes toward this new use of technology, as well as experience with online job search.

Ongoing career development is more important in the new economy for several reasons. First, as the earlier discussion of the diffusion of technology indicated, continued change is projected in the types of jobs that are in demand. Second, evidence from the past few decades reveals "an increasingly turbulent labor market" with few guarantees of job security.[34] Despite economic expansion in the 1990s, the job dislocation rate increased.[35] Corporate reengineering, relocation, and automation have exacerbated the churning of firms that some observers see as a hallmark and long-term attribute of the new economy.[36] Third, changing jobs represents a strategy for career mobility, as career ladders within firms are less prevalent than in the past.[37] Management positions often require a college degree, and some mid-level positions have disappeared, with responsibilities pushed downward in the organizational hierarchy.[38] Research on career mobility demonstrates that workers with high school diplomas who escape the low-wage threshold do so primarily by finding new jobs outside low-paying industries rather than through promotion within the low-wage sector.[39] Likewise, some studies indicate that former welfare recipients who voluntarily change jobs tend to have higher wages than those who persist in their original placement.[40]

Digital technology offers a new portal for career information and job search. For-profit websites such as Monster.com and Career-builder.com list hundreds of thousands of job openings and provide job seekers and employers with a variety of services. The "biggest and busiest job market in cyberspace" is America's Job Bank, sponsored by the U.S. Department of Labor.[41] The job bank lists more than a million openings and is linked to several companion websites collectively called "America's Career Kit." Through these partner sites and other links, job seekers can do all of the following online: research occupational requirements and salaries; find information on more than 350,000 training and educational programs; apply for admission and financial aid for a college program or a single web-based course; find advice on job search, interviewing, and resume writing; submit resumes; store applications in a customized database; receive automatic updates on jobs fitting their profile; and create customized searches by job title, geographic region, salary, and educational requirements. America's Job Bank includes jobs at all educational levels. A recent audit of the site turned up 550,000 jobs requiring a high school diploma or less.[42] Local workforce development efforts also employ information technology. San Diego's public jobs program has created a "virtual one-stop career center," where all transactions can be completed online.[43] Other public programs feature computerized resource centers that offer assistance for online job search and resume writing.[44]

Some proponents of government policy addressing the access divide have pointed to the job-networking potential of the Internet as an important reason for government intervention.[45] Casual acquaintances, or "weak ties" within personal networks, are valuable as informal referral systems for jobs.[46] Poor people living in areas of concentrated poverty often lack networks with sufficient information about jobs, particularly well-paying jobs. Because of residential segregation, low-income minority workers may be particularly disadvantaged and may be unable to find out about available jobs elsewhere in the metropolitan area.[47] In lieu of effective personal networks, workers are forced to rely on more formal mechanisms for job search, such as job-training programs, schools, classified ads, and employment services. This suggests that online job search may be particularly valuable for low-income and minority individuals.

Survey Results for Online Job Search

According to our survey, 30 percent of respondents have searched for or applied for a job online. A clear majority, 64 percent, said that they would feel comfortable using a computer for these purposes, so online job seekers may become more numerous in the future. Because limited access to computers and the Internet may have biased responses to the questions, we asked, "Would you use a computer located in a public place to search for or apply for a job online?" A public place was defined as a library or a community technology center, where computer access would be provided. The same proportion—64 percent—was willing to search for a job online, with or without public access.

Support for online job search was most likely among educated, young, male, and African American respondents, controlling for other factors.[48] Holding other demographic factors constant, the predicted probability of support for online job search was 14 percentage points higher for college graduates than for high school graduates. Similarly, the probability of support for online job search was 27 percentage points higher among younger respondents (defined as twenty-eight years old, or one standard deviation below the mean) compared to older respondents (defined as sixty-one years old, or one standard deviation above the mean). Racial and gender differences were smaller, but still statistically significant. The probability of favorable attitudes toward online job search was 77 percent for men compared to 70 percent for women and 76 percent for African Americans compared to 70 percent for whites, holding all other factors constant. Those who express interest in online job search are the technologically skilled,

WHAT MATTERS

Who Is More Willing to Search for a Job Online?

Young (81% for 28-year-olds vs. 54% for 61-year-olds)—27-point
    difference

Educated (76% for college graduate vs. 62% for high school diploma)—
    14-point difference

Males (77% vs. 70% for females)—7-point difference

African Americans (76% vs. 70% for whites)—6-point difference

Employed (70% vs. 63% for unemployed)—7-point difference

Who Is More Willing to Use Public Computer Access for Job Search?

African Americans

Educated

Males

Young

Who Is More Likely to Have Searched for a Job Online?

African Americans

Educated

Males

Young

Employed

Note: Estimates are based on a hypothetical respondent who is female, white, and
employed, with values for education, age, and income set at their mean for the
sample. The only statistically significant differences are the ones reported above
(see tables A4.2, A4.3, and A4.4). We have calculated the probability that respondents agree with these statements, controlling for other factors.

with the exception of African Americans. Income makes no difference in attitudes about online job search. These patterns remained
the same when we asked respondents whether they would be willing
to search for jobs using a computer located in a public place.[49] Public access did not make those lacking access more willing to engage in
online job search.

How do patterns regarding attitudes about Internet job search compare to actual experience? The same factors are statistically significant
predictors for use of online job search, with the exception that the

unemployed are statistically less likely to have searched for a job online than are employed respondents. Better-educated, younger, male, employed, and African American individuals are the most likely to have used the Internet for a job search, after controlling for other factors.[50]

Our findings are consistent with other surveys that have found that a higher percentage of African Americans have used the Internet for job search.[51] In our own survey, 37 percent of African Americans had searched for a job online, compared to only 28 percent of whites. The added value of our analysis is that we go beyond these simple percentages and find that the difference between African Americans and whites is statistically significant, controlling for other variables such as income, education, and age.

What could explain somewhat higher support for Internet job search, and markedly greater online job search activity, among African Americans? One explanation is that African Americans value additional network opportunities in particular, perhaps because they lack the informal networks that often serve as referral systems for job seekers. Interest in online job search and application is also consistent with African American perceptions about the connection between economic advancement and computer skills. This indicates a general willingness to use technology in pursuit of economic opportunity.

Lifelong Learning

Turbulence in the labor market and changing skills requirements also signal an increased need for continued training and education, or lifelong learning. Adult learners have many alternatives: vocational programs, degree-granting programs in community colleges and universities; adult basic education, including courses leading to a general education development (GED) credential, and on-the-job training, among others.

The trend over the past few decades has been toward a growing cohort of "nontraditional" adult students in colleges and universities. In fact, only "27 percent of today's undergraduates are 'traditional' students who have a high-school diploma, enroll full time right after high school, and depend on parents for financial support."[52]

Computers assist adult learners in two ways. First, they provide a useful tool for carrying out assignments in the traditional classroom.

Second, they have extended the walls of the classroom into the home and the community through web-based distance learning and educational software. In addition to the many distance-learning alternatives available through postsecondary institutions, web courses have made on-the-job training programs more convenient and cost effective for employers.[53]

The Organization for Economic Cooperation and Development (OECD) has urged member states to expand the use of distance learning for adult basic education programs focused on literacy and secondary education. Adult literacy programs enroll only about 10 percent of low-literacy Americans, and in all countries such programs have a high rate of turnover, with individuals frequently dropping in and out of classes.[54] Distance learning, according to the OECD, may ease the burden of managing education and adult responsibilities. There are other technological alternatives as well. Interactive software with self-paced drills can be used to develop basic skills such as literacy and numeracy. The Internet itself may serve as a teaching tool, encouraging individuals with limited literacy to increase their reading by following areas of interest. Limited home access and deficient computer skills present some hurdles for increasing distance learning and home study for adult basic education. Schools, libraries, and other institutions might use computers and the Internet to offer flexible options for independent study on their premises along with on-site technical and educational support.

Survey Results for Online Courses

In our survey, we asked respondents about their attitudes and experiences with online courses. As with online job search, more than two-thirds of respondents answered that they would be willing to take a class online. The percentage of respondents willing to take courses online was nearly identical to interest in online job search, but actual experience in distance learning was much more limited—11 percent had taken a course online versus 30 percent who had looked at job information on the Internet. Online courses obviously involve a higher commitment of time and money than online job search. Web-based courses can require information literacy and skills for use of bulletin boards or chat rooms, e-mail, file attachments, word processing, and streaming video. Technical glitches often require problem-solving abilities and patience. In fact, 53 percent of our respondents replied that they would need assistance in taking a course online. This was especially true for less-educated individuals. Of respondents without a high school diploma, 77 percent reported that they would need assistance to take a class online, and 57 percent of those with a high school diploma said they would need help. A substantial number of more-educated workers expressed a need for help, too—47 percent of those with some college, and 39 percent of those with a bachelor's or graduate degree.

Interestingly enough, substantially fewer individuals said that they would take an online course in a public place, where assistance could be offered. Only 53 percent of respondents were willing to do so, versus 61 percent of respondents who answered that they would take a course online. This 8-percentage-point drop contrasted with online job search, where public access made no difference. The more-sustained commitment of taking a course apparently made public access unattractive for some respondents. Even so, more than half of our respondents expressed a willingness to take a course through a public access site such as a library, community center, or school.

Interest in online education was statistically more likely among the educated, the young, the affluent, and the employed, controlling for other factors.[55] The pattern for online education diverged somewhat from attitudes about careers and job search, because interest was more consistent with the probability of access and skill. Income was a significant factor for interest in online courses, but it was not related to attitudes about careers or online job search. Age mattered, but not as much as for online job search. Interest in online education was only 10 percentage points higher for a hypothetical twenty-eight-year-old than for a sixty-one-year-old, compared to a 26-point difference for online job search.[56] Older respondents were more likely to be willing to take a course online than to search for a job online, reflecting higher interest in education than career development at this stage of life.

Although older, unemployed, less-educated, and low-income individuals are statistically less likely to express interest in web-based courses, there is still a high level of willingness to consider such an alternative, even among these less-interested groups. Translating this willingness into the commitment to actually take such classes is

WHAT MATTERS

Who Is More Willing to Take Online Courses?

Young (76% for 28-year-olds vs. 66% for 61-year-olds)—10-point difference

Educated (76% for college graduate vs. 66% for high school diploma)—10-point difference

Affluent (75% for high income vs. 65% for low income)—10-point difference

Employed (71% vs. 64% unemployed)—7-point difference

(Asian Americans and Latinos were less likely than whites to favor online courses.)

Who Is More Willing to Take an Online Course in a Public Place?

Young
Male
African American

Who Is More Likely to Have Taken Online Courses?

Young
Educated
Employed
African American

Note: Estimates are based on a hypothetical respondent who is female, white, and employed, with values for education, age, and income set at their mean for the sample. The only statistically significant differences are the ones reported above (see tables A4.2, A4.3, and A4.4). We have calculated the probability that respondents agree with the above statements, controlling for other factors.

another matter, however, in light of the need for assistance with computers expressed by many of these same groups, particularly the least educated.

Providing public access (and assistance) apparently did not make many disadvantaged groups more likely to cite interest in online classes—with one exception.[57] African Americans were more interested than whites in taking a class using a computer in a public place. Men are more willing than women to use public access sites for courses. The educated and the affluent drop out of the ranks of the "more interested" when online courses are located in a public place rather than being accessible from home.

Those who have actually taken classes online are statistically more likely to be young, better-educated, and employed, with the exception of African Americans, who were more likely than white respondents to have participated in online education.[58] This is consistent with the findings on online job searches.

To date, a small percentage of the population has actually participated in online courses. The options for online study are, however, expanding. The interest expressed by our respondents indicates potential for future growth as well.

Conclusion

Surveying the landscape of the new economy demonstrates clearly that information technology plays a role in economic opportunity. The word *opportunity* is key. Jobs will certainly be available, in the near and perhaps distant future, for individuals devoid of computer skills, but economic *opportunity* suggests the ability to subsist above the poverty level, to enjoy some choice and mobility in the labor market, and to realize higher returns for additional experience, skills, and training. An increasing number of jobs, including those for less-educated workers, require some type of computer use. Recent evidence, including our survey, suggests that even jobs requiring only a high school education sometimes involve rather sophisticated computer use beyond routine data entry, including navigation of the Internet. This may be particularly true for better-paying jobs and, as census data show, for mobility into supervisory and skilled jobs. Moreover, the boundaries of the landscape have rapidly changed over the past decade, and technology use in the workforce promises to continue to gain momentum. Computer use, however, cannot be considered in isolation from other dimensions of skill. The topography of the new economy indicates rising skills requirements overall, with increasing returns to education, and falling wages for the less-educated over much of the past few decades.

Our survey results demonstrate that more than two-thirds of Americans are convinced that a connection exists between computer skills and various types of economic opportunity. This is particularly true among disadvantaged groups such as African Americans, the unemployed, and women, as well as the young. African Americans and Latinos are even more likely than other racial and ethnic groups to believe that using the Internet is necessary to keep up with the times. This suggests that the policy problem is the inequitable distribution of opportunities for access and skills development rather than awareness of technology and its potential benefits.

Instability in the changing landscape of the new economy means that workers may need to change jobs more often, to respond to the threat of involuntary layoffs, or to pursue new prospects in the absence of well-defined career ladders. For many individuals, economic opportunity will entail job search and continued training and education. Technology offers new tools for obtaining information about jobs, for connecting with employers, and for enhancing skills and educational credentials. More than two-thirds of our respondents expressed a willingness to search for a job or take a course online, although only 30 percent have used the Internet to look for a job, and 11 percent have used it to take a class. Among those most willing to use the Internet for these purposes are those who are the most digitally savvy—respondents who are better-educated and young. Age differences are less stark for online education, although still significant. Income matters for online education, with the poor being less willing to take an online course, but it does not matter for attitudes about online job search or careers. Poor individuals apparently have many of the same attitudes and aspirations as other Americans regarding economic opportunity. Limited home access for the poor may present higher hurdles for online study than for online job search. A number of individuals also cited the need for assistance in taking an online course, especially the least educated.

Overall, income was not an important factor for the opportunity divide, at least not for attitudes about careers and online job search. The belief in technology and economic opportunity is widely shared, and groups more likely to suffer from technology skills deficits are at least as likely to believe that computer skills are necessary for economic opportunity.

What emerges from the survey is a depiction of African Americans as particularly attuned to the use of technology for economic opportunity. This is contrary to what would be expected, if a "digital divide" along the lines of race were a matter of attitudes rather than access and skills. This likely reflects a more general priority among African Americans regarding the need for economic opportunity, in view of the continued stark disparities in income. Despite economic progress over the past few decades, African Americans are still disproportionately represented among the poor. The median African American household income is only two-thirds that of white households.[59] Closing the income gap is not merely a matter of technological skills. Differences in educational attainment matter, too. So do other factors, such as segregation, the quality of education in central city neighborhoods, a "spatial mismatch" between the knowledge-intensive jobs available in central cities and the skills of inner-city residents, and discrimination by employers.[60] Still, the relatively widespread interest African Americans express in technology and economic advancement offers possibilities for closing the access and skills divides.

This favorable assessment of technological opportunity on the part of African Americans parallels other findings on racial attitudes about economic opportunity. A review of several decades of survey research concluded that, although African Americans perceived discrimination to be a serious problem, they were even more optimistic than white respondents about the future and their own chances for success in achieving the "American dream."[61] Poor African Americans were more likely than their middle-class counterparts to express their hopes for the future in terms of economic gains.[62]

Our findings build on these observations. In our heavily low-income sample, we discover a deep current of optimism about technology and economic opportunity among all respondents, but particularly among African Americans. Controlling for other factors, African Americans are more likely to believe that computer skills facilitate economic advancement, are more willing to use computers for job search (and actually use them more frequently than whites), and are also more willing to take courses online, when public access is provided (and to have taken online courses). These findings dovetail with some of the results in the prior chapter on the skills divide. African Americans were also more likely to agree to most methods of instruction or assistance, demonstrating a receptiveness beyond the generally favorable attitudes expressed by the majority of the sample. Latinos also expressed more positive attitudes than whites on some measures in this chapter and the previous one. For Latinos, however, the results were less consistent and less pronounced.

The focus in this chapter has been on individual aspirations for economic opportunity. Individual opportunities matter for public policy when systematic patterns of inequality rob some individuals of a fair chance for bettering their lot. Low levels of skill among the poor also have implications for welfare-to-work programs, if the goal of such initiatives is sustained employment sufficient to provide a standard of living above the poverty level; however, individual skills matter in a collective sense as well.

In the aggregate, skills and knowledge represent "human capital" for the development of the economy and society. Lester Thurow has characterized knowledge as "the new basis for wealth" in the information age.[63] The debate over skills in the early 1990s framed the problem as the need to maintain a nationally competitive economy amid the pressures of globalization and technological change. In recent years, state governments and business organizations have defined educational issues as economic development concerns.[64] Impoverished rural communities and cities suffering from deindustrialization have likewise turned toward human capital strategies, hoping to attract new industries, including high-tech firms, on the basis of a skilled, educated workforce.[65] By addressing the divide in technological skills together with the need for other training and education, public policy can take steps to ensure opportunities for individuals and for their communities.

Notes

1. See Castells 2000, 77; Niskanen 2000, 93; U.S. Department of Commerce 2000a, 1; McGuckin and Van Ark 2001, 10.

2. U.S. Department of Commerce 2002; Pew Internet and American Life Project 2000.

3. Mishel, Bernstein, and Schmitt 2001, 19–20; Barrington 2000.

4. Organization for Economic Cooperation and Development 2000, 3.

5. Mishel, Bernstein, and Schmitt 2001, 154.

6. Atkinson and Court 1998, 25; Bernhardt et al. 2001, 48; Ellwood 2000.

7. Mishel, Bernstein, and Schmitt 2001, 1; U.S. Department of Labor 1999, 5; Ellwood 2000, 31.

8. Barrington 2000, 8.

9. Mishel, Bernstein, and Schmitt 2001, 1.

10. Census bureau figures for 2001, reported in Pear 2002.

11. Carnevale and Rose 2001, 52.

12. Kruse and Blasi 2000.

13. Carnevale and Rose 2001, 64; Strawn and Martinson 2001, 111.

14. Bernhardt et al. 2001, 133.

15. Herzenberg, Alic, and Wial 1998, 63.

16. McGuckin and Van Ark 2001; U.S. Department of Labor 1999, chap. 2.

17. U.S. Department of Commerce 2002, 57.

18. See, for example, Moss and Tilly 2001, and Holzer 1996.

19. According to the 1997 National Employer Survey, nonsupervisory workers were engaged in computer use at 52 percent of firms—up from 42 percent in 1994 (Kruse and Blasi 2000, 72). A telephone survey of employers in several major cities revealed that computers were used in nearly 59 percent of jobs not requiring a bachelor's degree. They were reportedly used on a daily basis in 51 percent of these non-college jobs (Holzer 1996, 49).

20. Holzer 1996, 49; Kruse and Blasi 2000, 72; Moss and Tilly 2001, 83.

21. The rest of the ten occupations with the largest expected growth include computer-related professions, such as computer support and software engineers, and jobs likely to involve some computer use, such as office clerks, customer service representatives, and registered nurses.

22. U.S. Department of Commerce 2002, 58, 60. For the category of operators, fabricators, and laborers, only 20.7 percent reported using computers at work, and, of them, 9.2 percent used the Internet or e-mail at work. This was the lowest category for computer use, with service workers reporting only a slighter higher percentage of computer use, at 25.4 percent. For more-skilled workers with specialized training, the rates of usage are higher. For the category of precision production, craft, and repair, computer use rose to 31.7 percent.

23. Technology can result in either deskilling or upskilling of jobs. The introduction of optical scanners, for example, has lowered the skills requirements for cashier jobs, because it reduced the need for mathematical skills. Most analysts argue that skills requirements have risen in the new economy (Holzer 1996, 2–3; Teixeira and McGranahan 1998, 120–21; Kruse and Blasi 2000, 55, 128; Moss and Tilly 2001, 49, 56; Osterman 2001, 75) on the basis of evidence from the National Employer Survey and other research. The 1994 National Employer Survey revealed that 56 percent of employers experienced an increase in the required skills for production or support jobs

over the prior three years (Kruse and Blasi 2000, 55, 128). Studies of both urban and rural areas have found that between 30 and 40 percent of jobs in these economically distressed areas have experienced some upskilling in noncollege occupations (Holzer 1996, 49; Teixeira and McGranahan 1998, 121; Moss and Tilly 2001, 56, 83).

24. Moss and Tilly 2001, 65.

25. Holzer 1996, 49; Moss and Tilly 2001, 56, 83; Teixeira and McGranahan 1998, 121–23.

26. Osterman 1999, 108; U.S. Department of Labor 1999.

27. Herzenberg, Alic, and Wial 1998, 63; Appelbaum and Albin 1998, 155–56.

28. Secretary's Commission on Achieving Necessary Skills 1992, 10–11.

29. Osterman 2001, 74.

30. Teixeira and McGranahan 1998, 123.

31. Because the dependent variable is binary for the model "it is necessary for people to use the Internet to keep up with the times," logistic regression coefficients are reported in table A4.1.

32. Since the dependent variable for this economic opportunity index is measured on an ordinal scale, coefficients are based on an ordered logistic regression model. See table A4.1.

33. Hall and Mervis 1995, 323; Herzenberg, Alic, and Wial 1998, 5.

34. Osterman 1999, 53.

35. Osterman 1999, 48; Kruse and Blasi 2000, 44.

36. Atkinson and Court 1998, 5.

37. Bernhardt et al. 2001, 192; Herzenberg, Alic, and Wial 1998, 13.

38. Herzenberg, Alic, and Wial 1998.

39. Bernhardt et al. 2001, 167–68.

40. Strawn and Martinson (2001) cite Cancian and Meyer (2000), Gladden and Taber (2000), and Rangarajan, Schochet, and Chu (1998). The latter is available online at www.mathinc.com.

41. See www.ajb.org.

42. Stiglitz, Orszag, and Orszag 2000, 85.

43. See Heldrich Center 2002.

44. See Heldrich Center 2002; Saulny 2001.

45. Civille 1995, 198–99.

46. Civille 1995, 198–99; Osterman 2001, 78.

47. Civille 1995, 198–99; Moss and Tilly 2001, 254; Holzer 1996, 127–28; Kasarda 1990.

48. Because the dependent variable is binary, logistic regression coeffi-

cients are reported in table A4.2. We calculate predicted probabilities for all variables holding other factors constant (King, Tomz, and Wittenberg 2000). Our hypothetical individual has average (mean) education, age, and income and is an employed white female.

49. For results, see table A4.3.

50. Because the dependent variable is binary, logistic regression coefficients are reported in table A4.4.

51. The Pew Internet and American Life Project study (2000) showed that 51 percent of African Americans who have ever used the Internet have used it to get information about jobs, compared to 37 percent of whites who had ever used the Internet.

52. Evelyn 2002.

53. Greengard 1998.

54. Ginsburg, Sabatini, and Wagner 2000, 78–79.

55. For results, see table A4.2.

56. All predicted probabilities are calculated holding other factors constant (King, Tomz, and Wittenberg 2000). Again, our hypothetical individual has average (mean) education, age, and income and is an employed white female.

57. For results, see table A4.3.

58. For results, see table A4.4.

59. The 2001 median household income was $29,470 for African Americans and $46,305 for whites. See U.S. Census 2002b.

60. Holzer 1996, 127–28; Moss and Tilly 2001, 254; Kasarda 1990.

61. Hochschild 1995, 69.

62. Ibid., 73.

63. Thurow 1999, xv.

64. Mickelson 1996, 246; Sipple et al. 1997.

65. Swaim, Gibbs, and Teixeira 1998, xi; Clarke and Gaile 1998, chap. 7; Johnson 2002.

Chapter 5

The Democratic Divide

with Ramona McNeal

I n an era when the outcome of a presidential election is decided by a few hundred votes, and the balance of power in the U.S. Senate can be determined by a similarly close margin, the question of what effect the Internet as a medium for political information and involvement has on the voting public is a pertinent one. The Internet may enhance citizen information about elections and in turn stimulate increased participation. Yet, because of unequal access to technology, the Internet may expand turnout rates only among those who are already predisposed to vote, broadening the gulf between those who do and those who do not participate. In light of declining civic engagement and participation in American politics in the last three decades, the question of what effects new information technology may have on democracy is ever more important.[1]

Leading theories of political participation have shown that socioeconomic characteristics of voters—education and income—are the most important factors in explaining whether one votes in the United States. Voter turnout is also affected by race, age, gender, and attitudinal factors such as strength of partisanship, political efficacy, and political interest.[2] Although a long tradition of research documents the demographic and psychological determinants of political participation, there is also evidence to suggest that changes in communication technology may play an important role in influencing electoral behavior. Research has found that those who read about politics in newspapers learn more than those who watch television.[3] In the past decade, technology has changed the way many people gather news and participate in politics. The most important of these new technologies is the Internet, which has become the mass medium for the twenty-first century. The Internet combines the audiovisual components of traditional forms of media such as newspaper and television with the interactivity and speed of telephone and mail. It facilitates flexibility, allowing individuals to choose what information to access and when to access it. Technology also permits users to exchange large amounts of information quickly, regardless of distance.

A limited but developing body of research has explored the relationship between Internet use and varying forms of civic participation, including voting.[4] Few researchers, however, have explored citizen attitudes toward the use of information technology for political participation and communication with government. We are most interested in attitudes because of their potential to affect participation in the future, as nascent trends toward online government and politics build momentum. Is there a "democratic divide" that emerges from the access and skill divides? Are more-educated, affluent citizens more supportive of using the Internet for political participation than those with lower socioeconomic status? A lack of access and computer skills may negatively influence attitudes about using computers and the Internet to communicate with government and participate in politics. In an era when "e-government" is rapidly spreading and the use of Internet voting may well be on the horizon, the answers to these questions have clear implications for public policy as well as future political participation.

Some scholars suggest the Internet may function as a new deliberative public forum, drawing the less engaged into civic life, strengthening democracy, increasing political participation, and leveling the playing field. Others claim that the "digital divide" and the growing corporate ownership of the Internet will merely replicate the patterns of inequality experienced today. Davis contends powerful groups will continue to dominate the production of political news and information, the expression of opinion, and the mobilization of political participation, online as well as off.[5] The literature on traditional political participation already shows a substantial gap based on income and education.[6] This research addresses whether practices such as online voting and e-government will exacerbate or ameliorate existing disparities in political participation based on demographic factors. Alongside some hopeful signs, our data do reveal a democratic divide,

as individuals with higher education and income are more supportive of digital democracy.

Theories of Digital Democracy

Many scholars and political pundits argue that Americans are becoming more and more disenchanted with traditional institutions of representative government and disillusioned with older forms of civic
engagement and participation. Although a "crisis of democracy" may
be overstated, indicators suggest an increasing number of "critical
citizens" are characterized by high expectations of democracy as an
ideal yet low evaluations of the actual performance of representative
institutions.[7]

Participation has become one of the dominant themes of modern
governance.[8] Normative theorists in particular have long argued that
direct forms of democracy can motivate participation by energizing
citizens with a sense of civic duty and political efficacy.[9] For advocates
of direct democracy, such as Benjamin Barber, opportunities and
mechanisms are needed to increase citizen deliberation and direct
involvement in decision making, for example, through initiatives and
referendums. Calling for more "discursive democracy," "strong
democracy," "teledemocracy," and "deliberation," scholars have
offered a variety of participatory models of decision making.[10] From
radical models of a pure direct democracy to more transparent representative systems, citizen participation is deemed as critical in governing accountability and public dialogue.[11]

These participatory models imply that the system of representative
democracy is far from perfect in transmitting the wishes of the public into policy and that citizen participation can improve politics and
policy, even in a complex modern society.[12] The general prescription
for making government function better is to foster greater individual
and collective participation and structure institutions to include mass
citizen participation. In its simplest form, participatory government
is plebescitarian, with the public being asked to decide public issues
by a direct vote.[13]

Some scholars see information technology as the most important
ingredient for fueling a participatory revolution.[14] Proponents argue
that the democratizing effect of the Internet will encourage citizen

participation at all levels of government. The interactivity, low-cost, flexibility, and information capacity available on the Internet have the potential to allow the public to become more knowledgeable about politics as a first step toward greater participation. New information technologies generate multiple opportunities for sharing political information and communication. Chat rooms, listservs, e-mail, and bulletin board systems represent new modes of information exchange and opinion mobilization. By allowing individuals to be both receivers and active providers of information, the Internet may foster increased political communication. As a new channel of two-way communication, the Internet may strengthen and enrich connections between citizens, on the one hand, and political parties, interest groups, and elected officials, on the other.[15] Proponents of e-democracy argue that the Internet offers hope to reconnect citizens to the political process and revive civic engagement in American politics.[16]

To date, the Internet has mostly provided a conduit for information and communication. In the future, the Internet may offer new opportunities for participation through online registration and voting, virtual town meetings, and petition drives that utilize electronic signatures. Some suggest that those states that have been leaders in using direct democracy will be the first to allow Internet voting and voter registration. Two unsuccessful citizen initiatives circulated for the 2000 California ballot, for example, would have required the secretary of state to implement Internet voting and voter registration.[17] Arizona, a state with frequent use of ballot initiatives and referenda, was the first to hold a binding election using Internet voting in 2000.[18]

Others, however, contend that information technology will promote further inequality in democratic participation, widening the gap between those who participate and those who do not.[19] Individuals with higher income and education are already statistically more likely to vote in the United States.[20] Disparities in access to the Internet based on income, education, race, and ethnicity mean that technology resources are far from equally distributed and that online politics may therefore amplify the voice of the affluent and well educated, further marginalizing the underprivileged. In this scenario, opportunities for online political participation will primarily benefit those elites with the resources and motivation to take advantage of them, leaving the poor and uneducated farther behind.[21]

Research on the Internet
and Political Participation

How does empirical research inform this largely normative debate? Early studies on the effects of the Internet on civic engagement have been mixed. Using a national representative sample from the 1998 American National Election Surveys, Bimber found that access to the Internet had no impact on voter participation.[22] With the exception of giving campaign donations, the political behavior of those with access to the Internet and online political information did not differ from those who did not use the Internet to seek political information. Access to the Internet and online political information did statistically increase the probability that a respondent would contribute money to political campaigns, suggesting a mobilizing potential. Bimber's research, however, is limited to one midterm election.

Recent research, using more sophisticated statistical methods and longitudinal datasets, concluded that the use of the Internet for political information had a positive effect on participation during recent presidential elections. Tolbert and McNeal found the Internet may enhance information about candidates and elections, and in turn stimulate increased participation.[23] Using National Election Study (NES) data from 1986–2000, they observed that respondents with access to the Internet and online political news were significantly more likely to have voted in the 1996 and 2000 presidential elections. This raises the question, however, of whether the Internet influenced political participation or whether political activists happened to be more likely to be online. The authors used a two-stage model to isolate cause and effect (to control for simultaneity problems) and used multivariate regression to hold factors other than Internet use constant. Participation increased even after controlling for education, income, race/ethnicity, gender, age, partisanship, attitudes, traditional media use, and state environmental factors. The exception to this pattern was the 1998 midterm election, the year studied by Bimber. Simulations suggest Internet access increased the probability of voting by an average of 12 percent, and use of online election information increased the probability of voting by 7.5 percent in the 2000 election, all else equal. The mobilizing potential of the Internet in 2000 was also associated with other forms of involvement in election campaigns.

Individuals viewing online political information were significantly more likely to talk to others about candidates or parties, display buttons or signs, work for a party or candidate, attend rallies, and give money to candidates, parties, and interest groups.

Other studies have addressed the information and communication potential of the Internet for influencing political participation, including activities such as contacting political officials, attending rallies, or signing petitions. Weber and Bergman found that those individuals who engaged in Internet activities such as using e-mail and chat-rooms were more likely to be engaged in a variety of political activities.[24] Weber and Bergman, however, used *Survey 2000,* an online survey jointly conducted by academic researchers and National Geographic Interactive. The survey was self-selected and nonrandom and therefore subject to selection bias, unlike the studies reported above. One nationally representative survey (1999 DDB Life Style Study) contrasted Internet use for information exchange to use for social recreation, product consumption, or financial management. Across age cohorts (generation X and baby boomers) individuals who used the Internet for information exchange reported higher levels of interpersonal trust and civic engagement, after controlling for demographic, contextual, and traditional media use variables.[25]

Another area of participation that has been singled out by researchers for study is citizen-initiated contact of public officials. Earlier research found that age, gender, education, political connectedness, and proximity to government institutions are important factors in determining whether a citizen will initiate communication. Older, educated, white citizens have been found to be more likely to contact government officials, whereas women were less likely to instigate contact.[26] Utilizing a self-selected, nonrandom online survey conducted in 1996 and 1997 and two phone surveys, Bimber examined whether the Internet altered the pattern of citizen communication.[27] He found that, when comparing traditional means of communication to the Internet, many of the same relations still existed. The Internet, however, magnified the gender gap in communication but narrowed the difference based on political connectedness. Despite the limitations of Bimber's nonrandom sample, his study was one of the few to explore the demographic impact of new modes of communication.

Research on the Emerging Issue
of Internet Voting

One of the controversies over the possible introduction of Internet voting is its differential impact, in light of disparities in access. An analysis of the 2000 online Arizona Democratic primary offers a window into how changing election procedures to accommodate digital technology may change election outcomes.[28] The 2000 primary allowed registered Democratic voters to cast ballots in four ways: 41.16 percent used the Internet; 37.68 percent used traditional absentee mail ballots; 4.8 percent used electronic voting machines at polling booths; and 16.36 percent used paper ballots. Based on a pre- and postelection survey funded by the National Science Foundation, Solop found that better-educated and younger voters took advantage of the Internet voting option in the Arizona primary.[29] Education has already been found to be an important factor in determining whether individuals choose to participate in politics. Inclusion of an Internet alternative may further bias voting patterns toward the higher educated. Younger voters, however, have historically been among those groups least likely to participate. Online voting may be instrumental in increasing turnout among the young.

Alvarez and Nagler argue that one way to assess Internet voting is to compare the group of citizens currently voting to those that would vote if online balloting were implemented.[30] Sharp differences in the demographics of these two groups would be evidence of a change in political representation caused by Internet voting. Alvarez and Nagler use aggregate census and election return data from Arizona's fifteen counties and ecological-inference methods to estimate white and nonwhite Democratic turnout rates.[31] They compare turnout in the 1998 statewide Democratic primary with the 2000 Democratic presidential primary, where Internet voting was introduced. Although overall statewide turnout was significantly lower in the 2000 primary (10.59 percent) compared to average primary turnout of 23.94 percent in the past three elections, the authors find that the average rate of decrease for nonwhite voters was six times greater than the average rate of decrease for white voters. White turnout actually increased from 1998 levels in two counties, but nonwhite turnout declined from 1998 to 2000 in every Arizona county.[32]

The research on Internet voting suggests its potential to mobilize new sectors of the population, particularly the young, but also to expand existing disparities in participation rates based on race and ethnicity. A number of factors, however, make it difficult to generalize from the Arizona case study to other state and national elections. There is an inherent difficulty in comparing turnout in an off-year (1998) and a presidential (2000) election. There are some problems with using statistical methods in this particular study, where the number of "things" being studied—counties—is not very large.[33] The unique circumstances of the Arizona election also cast some doubt on its broader implications. The national Democratic contest had already been decided by the time of the Arizona primary, resulting in extremely depressed turnout. It may have been this, rather than Internet voting, that caused turnout rates to plummet among some groups more than others.

Initial findings about Internet voting are suggestive, but Internet voting may not be a widespread reality in the near future. Controversies over e-voting include concerns about election fraud and online privacy, and the construction of secure voting systems would entail considerable expense.[34] Some states already allow online voter registration,[35] and Georgia allows absentee ballots to be cast online. Electronic government, however, represents a technology application that is currently burgeoning and that, according to its advocates, has the potential to transform the relationship between citizens and government at all levels—local, state, and federal.

Theories of E-Government

E-government "refers to the delivery of information and services online via the Internet or other digital means," and may also include opportunities for online political participation.[36] The diffusion of e-government has been rapid and widespread. The federal government has emphasized the creation of federal websites as part of its effort to "reinvent" government, and there is now a central portal for all federal services.[37] All fifty states have adopted some form of e-government; a recent survey indicates that 80 percent of local governments maintain websites.[38]

E-government is characterized by multiple constituencies and multiple goals. Streamlining government-to-business transactions, such as procurement and permits, is one aim of e-government, and the traditional orientation of state and municipal websites has been to promote business and economic development.[39] Our primary concern in discussing the relationship between e-government and a democratic divide is "government-to-citizen" transactions.[40] E-government is most relevant to ordinary citizens for its potential to improve service delivery and to enhance transparency and responsiveness of government agencies.[41] Proponents argue that e-government could enable citizens to interact with and receive services from government twenty-four hours a day, seven days a week. They describe e-government as "the continuous optimization of service delivery, constituency participation, and governance by transforming internal and external relationships through technology, the Internet and new media."[42] E-government initiatives are an outgrowth of the reinventing government paradigm, particularly at the federal level, that were promoted by the Clinton-Gore administration.[43] Goals touted by the administration included increased efficiency, responsiveness to "customers," and citizen empowerment.[44] Others suggest e-government has grown larger than government reform and carries with it expectations and possibilities of transforming, not just reforming, government, consistent with the literature on digital democracy.[45]

What, in practice, does e-government look like?[46] At its most basic level, e-government consists of the posting of information about services, contact persons, and a variety of government documents, including forms, policies, and legislation. At a more sophisticated level, it allows completion of government transactions online. The federal government now permits electronic filing of income tax forms, and about 25 percent of federal and state websites offer online transactions for services such as vehicle registration, driver's licenses, hunting and fishing licenses, tax filing, and more.[47] Service delivery improvements may include portals or "one-stop" websites that centralize services and information through links and perhaps searchable databases. The federal job bank described in the previous chapter is an example of e-government services delivered entirely online. Such transactions are less frequently available on local government websites.[48] To realize their potential for making government more accessible, websites may need to do more than centralize information online. Some research points to a need to clarify legal and technical terminology on government websites and to organize and present information in ways that are user friendly.[49] This may be particularly important for individuals with limited education or experience with contacting government agencies or following legislation.

Many observers view e-government as a means for enhancing democratic participation, as government information online promotes transparency.[50] The Internet also facilitates communication with agencies and elected officials, especially through e-mail. Eighty-four percent of federal and state websites include e-mail addresses, and government receipt of e-mail from constituents is increasing.[51] Online public hearings and forums have the potential to allow interaction on a broader scale and to encourage deliberative participation. These broader forms of technology-enabled participation are fairly rare. Only 15 percent of federal and state websites provide message boards for public comment, and less than 1 percent offer real-time chat rooms.[52] The end of this chapter discusses Berkeley, California's, experiment with an online forum during the revisions of the city's master plan. Other forays into technologically enabled participation have been tried at the community level in the past. Santa Monica, California, used its Public Electronic Network and public access sites for both community information and citizen participation prior to the advent of the Internet. In general, however, government-sponsored or -sanctioned initiatives for electronic participation have been rare. As the Berkeley case study indicates, such use confronts a number of legal and logistical problems as well as disparities in citizen access to the Internet.

The ambiguous nature of e-government, like digital democracy, has resulted in hype and confusion with little systematic consideration of the expectations and limitations of taking government online.[53] Discussions of e-government are wrapped in the language of increasing citizen participation, but the reality is that the posting of information and service delivery are more prevalent than efforts to promote participation. Surveys of state and local officials show that most of them view e-government in terms of its potential to increase efficiency and cut costs.[54] Other studies explore the causes promoting the spread of e-government and find that citizen demand, measured by Internet access in the state, is not a significant explanation for innovation in e-government. Controlling for other factors, states with Republican-controlled legislatures, more professional networks, and higher levels of legislative professionalization are likely to engage in more extensive use of e-government. This research also implies efficiency needs drive reliance on e-government rather than concerns about expanding political participation.[55] This is consistent with other recent government reforms, such as "reinventing" government. At the federal level, the reinvention effort emphasized cost reduction and efficiency over other stated goals such as citizen empowerment and responsiveness.[56]

Service delivery and efficiency concerns are likely to dominate further development of e-government.[57] Yet, even if all the starry-eyed predictions for its potential do not come to pass, e-government has so far demonstrated important benefits for citizens. First, it can provide valuable access to information about government services. Websites can eliminate the need to travel to government offices to obtain government forms or other documents. Searchable databases, lists of frequently asked questions, and links to related sites can make information easily accessible and convenient when it is provided and presented in an understandable fashion. Low-income citizens often depend heavily upon various government services and could benefit from better access to information. Second, e-government has contributed to communication and accountability, although it falls short of the prescriptions of e-democracy proponents. Wider availability of information and the increased use of e-mail can facilitate civic awareness and interaction with officials. There are other means, of course, to obtain information and to contact officials, but they can involve frustrating trips from office to office and long delays of telephone tag. Access to e-government for all is a desirable public objective.

To date, there are a few initial studies on the public's use of e-government sites. The Pew Internet and American Life project surveys describe use of government information as one of the fastest-growing online activities in recent years. Of those who use the Internet, 58 percent have visited at least one government website, making this one of the most popular Internet uses.[58] Two surveys show that e-government users are likely to be younger, better-educated, and more affluent, although neither of these studies controls for other factors using multivariate regression.[59] Both surveys also indicate that African Americans are somewhat more likely than whites to visit local government websites, which are otherwise the least used.[60]

Of those accessing online government information, 77 percent seek information on tourism or recreation, 70 percent conduct research for work or school, 63 percent download government forms, 63 percent look for information about services an agency provides, and 62 percent gather information on policies or issues. In terms of transactions, 16 percent of those who seek online government information are filing taxes, 12 percent are renewing a driver's license or car registration, and 7 percent are renewing a professional license. A smaller proportion (4 percent) is seeking a fishing, hunting, or recreation license, and 2 percent are paying a fine. The Pew survey data reveal that e-government is well underway, in contrast to online voting.

Some research is beginning to accumulate in the area of e-government more generally, but so far only a few studies address citizen use and attitudes. Like much of the research on the access divide, these studies often lack statistical controls, which would impart more confidence in their findings, and representative samples of the poor and minorities. The existing research on the Internet and political participation is more developed, but still limited. Studies are often based on single elections or nonrandom samples, limiting our ability to draw broad conclusions. Our research on attitudes may provide a better predictor of the way in which the Internet will affect political awareness and engagement in the near future. Are citizens supportive of e-government and possible future reforms to implement Internet voting and online voter registration? How do citizens feel about using the Internet for town meetings? By examining attitudes, we can find out whether disadvantaged groups see access to e-government as an important need and whether there is popular support for participatory reforms such as Internet voting, online voter registration, and town meetings in the future.

Findings from the Survey

Will use of the Internet for political participation expand or ameliorate the existing disparities in traditional participation in American politics? Analysis of our survey data suggest both the potential of online politics to expand civic participation among some who are currently disengaged from politics as well as the potential to widen existing disparities in participation based on income and education.

Simple percentages from our survey demonstrate that many who have Internet access do not use it for political purposes and that some innovations, such as online voting, are controversial. In comparison to the 54 percent who had home Internet access and 58 percent who had e-mail addresses, 31 percent of respondents had searched for political information online, but only 17 percent had seen an online political ad. There was somewhat more interest in e-government than in obtaining political information—40 percent of all respondents had looked up information on government services online.

Respondents expressed resounding support for putting government information online but were more reticent about using the Internet for voting and online town meetings. More than three-quarters of respondents (78 percent) answered positively to the question, "How do you feel about looking up government information online?" This exceeded the two-thirds majorities who said they were willing to search for a job or take a class online. These attitudes confirm the popularity of e-government suggested by the Pew study of current use. Support for Internet voting was almost evenly split. When asked, "How do you feel about voting in a government election online?" 48 percent agreed and 52 percent were opposed. This could indicate public qualms about this particular reform (security or privacy), or more general disinterest in voting. The survey revealed more support for online voter registration. When asked, "How do you feel about registering to vote online?" support rose to 58 percent. Support for participating in an online political forum was modest as well: only 47 percent of individuals responded positively to the question, "How do you feel about participating in an online town meeting?" It is possible that our findings were skewed by the abundant presence of either voters or nonvoters, but, when we controlled for reported voting in traditional elections, support for the varying forms of digital government remained virtually the same.

Because limited access to computers and the Internet may have biased responses to the online participation question, we repeated the questions asking whether the respondent supported use of information technology for voting, registration, and looking up government information using a computer in a public place. In this case, access would be provided and election fraud could be more easily controlled. When asked, "Would you use a computer located in a public place to vote in an election?" support rose by more than 10 percentage points, with 59 percent agreeing. Sixty-seven percent of respondents supported using a computer in a public place to register to vote, and 74 percent supported using a computer to search for information on government services. As with job search and taking a course online, respondents were slightly less willing to seek government information using public access. They were, however, considerably more willing to use new technology for voting and registration at a public place rather than at home. Even with a representative sample of low-income individuals, the majority of respondents were supportive of digital democracy and e-government, at least when public access (and security) is provided.

Support for Digital Democracy and E-Government

Using multivariate regression, we compared the results of four models. In light of the differing levels of support for e-government versus voting online, we developed a separate model to explain support for each of the following: (1) voting in a government election online; (2) registering to vote online; (3) looking up government information online; and (4) participating in an online town meeting. The responses for each question were coded 1 for agree and 0 for disagree.[61] We also created an index of support for online politics and government overall that combined items 1 through 4.

The same explanatory factors used in the access divide analysis are included in the appendix tables for this chapter, with one exception. We added a measure of traditional political participation, where 1 indicates that the individual was both registered for and voted in the 2000 presidential election and 0 otherwise. This measure was created by combining two survey questions and was used instead of voting to help control for the problem of overreporting in survey data. The problem with using self-reported voting alone is that the percentage of people who ostensibly vote usually far outstrips actual turnout. The results are explained in the What Matters box that follows, and the regression tables are provided in appendix 1.

Although overall support for the differing forms of political participation varied significantly—from a low of 48 percent for online voting to a high of 78 percent for searching for government information online—factors associated with support for digital democracy

WHAT MATTERS

1. **Who Is More Likely to Support Online Voting?**
   Educated, young, Democrats, voted in 2000 elections

2. **Who Is More Likely to Support Online Voter Registration?**
   Educated, young, Democrats, males, voted in 2000 elections

3. **Who Is More Likely to Support E-Government (Looking Up Government Information Online)?**
   Educated, affluent, young, Democrats, non-Latino, voted in 2000 elections

4. **Who Is More Likely to Support Participating in an Online Town Meeting?**
   Educated, affluent, young, males, voted in 2000 elections

5. **Who Is More Likely to Support Digital Democracy and E-Government Overall (questions 1–4 combined)?**
   Educated, affluent, young, Democrats, males, voted in 2000 elections

Note: The only statistically significant differences are reported above (see tables A5.1 and A5.2). When multivariate regression is used, these are the variables that matter, holding other factors constant.

and e-government are surprisingly similar (see table A5.1). What emerges from the data is clear evidence telling a single story—a democratic divide exists in support for online politics and government. After controlling for other factors, the respondents most likely to favor online politics and government are younger, better educated and more affluent, and are more likely to take part in traditional forms of political participation (voted in the 2000 election). Although there were no significant differences in attitudes toward online voting or registering based on income, the poor have more negative attitudes about e-government—participating in an electronic town meeting or searching for government information online—than did those with higher incomes. This represents a significant downside to the groundswell of interest in e-government. Surveys that trace only these general trends are not able to isolate significant differences in the groups responding to innovations like e-government. The benefits of e-government—easy access to information about government policies, community activities, and services—may be largely untapped by the poor, even though they are more likely than higher-income individuals to depend upon public services. Partisan differences also surface: Democrats were more supportive of online voting, registering to vote, and accessing online government information than were independents or Republicans. This is noteworthy, because Democrats are less likely to have access to the Internet than Republicans (see chapter 2).

Gender appeared as an important factor: men were statistically more willing than women to register to vote online and take part in online town meetings. This gender gap finding is consistent with that of Bimber, who found that women were less likely to use the Internet to initiate contact with public officials.[62] Although men are more likely than women to have e-mail addresses (as reported in chapter 2), attitudes about politics rather than technology may be driving gender differences. Factors other than access are also important when assessing the potential impact of information technology on public policy.

We find that race and ethnicity are not significant factors in predicting attitudes toward online political participation. African Americans, Latinos, and Asian Americans do not differ significantly from similarly situated whites in support for digital democracy.[63] Latinos were statistically less likely to be willing to search for government information online, but otherwise there are no differences. Although the access divide is clearly characterized by racial and ethnic disparities, the democratic divide, for the most part, is not.

We further explored the results for online voting and registration using predicted probabilities to compare the magnitude of income, education, and age in shaping support for online politics.[64] Because voting is the most basic component of participation in a democracy and previous surveys have not explored attitudes toward online voting and registration, the responses to these questions have special significance.

The two factors that have the greatest substantive impact on support for online voting and registration are education and age. Holding other demographic factors constant, support for online voting and online registration were 19 and 22 percentage points higher among individuals with a college degree than for those with only a high school diploma. This mirrors existing disparities in civic participation, which are largely associated with educational differences. Age

WHAT MATTERS

Who Is More Likely to Support Online Voting?

Educated (59% college degree vs. 40% high school diploma)—19-point difference

Young (60% for 28-year-olds vs. 41% for 61-year-olds)—19-point difference

Democrats (50% vs. 40% for Republicans)—10-point difference

Who Is More Likely to Support Online Voter Registration?

Educated (67% college degree vs. 47% high school diploma)—20-point difference

Young (71% for 28-year-olds vs. 45% for 61-year-olds)—26-point difference

Democrats (59% vs. 52% for Republicans)—7-point difference

Males (65% vs. 59% for females)—6-point difference

Note: Estimates are based on a hypothetical respondent who is female, white, and independent, with values for education, age, and income set at their mean for the sample. The only statistically significant differences are reported above (see table A5.1). We have calculated the probability that respondents agree with the above statements, controlling for other factors.

was equally important. The simulations show a 19 percent decreased probability in supporting online voting and a 26 percent decreased probability in supporting online registration when moving from the young (twenty-eight years old, one standard deviation below the mean) to the old (sixty-one years old, one standard deviation above the mean).

Compared to age and education, gender had a smaller impact on attitudes toward online participation and was statistically significant only for attitudes toward online voter registration. After holding other factors constant, females were 6 percent less likely to favor online voter registration than were males. Income, race, and ethnicity do not drive attitudes about online voting and registration, holding other demographic factors constant. Partisanship, however, resulted in significant and interesting differences. Although Democrats were least likely to have Internet access (54 percent), they were most likely to favor online voting (50 percent) and registration (59 percent). Republicans were most likely to have access (64 percent) and less favorable toward digital politics. Independents were least likely to favor online voting (39 percent) and online registration (50 percent).

Finally, we examined support for online participation in a public location and current political activity online.[65] We created an index of support for participation in a public place (where public access and security could be provided) in regard to voting, registering to vote, and looking up government information online. These questions allow us to compensate for reluctance to participate online that is due to the need for computer access, assistance, or security concerns.

As discussed previously, respondents were generally more supportive of online participation in a public place. The findings reveal that young, educated, higher-income, and male respondents, as well as those who participate in traditional politics, are more willing to participate in online political activities in a public place. Public access does not change attitudes about participation for groups that are disadvantaged in terms of access or skills, but partisanship emerges as an important factor. Paradoxically, while Democrats were more supportive of online voting and registration in general, Republicans were more likely to support use of computers and the Internet for voting in a public location. This suggests Republicans may be more concerned with security issues than Democrats. Overall the data reveal significantly lower support for online voting, registration, and e-government by

WHAT MATTERS

Who Is More Likely to Support Online Voting and Registration in a Public Place?

Educated, affluent, young, male, Republican, voted in 2000 elections

Who Is More Likely to Participate Online Now?

Educated, affluent, young, male, voted in 2000 elections

Note: The only statistically significant differences are reported above (see table A5.2). When multivariate regression is used, these are the variables that matter, holding other factors constant.

those with lower incomes, lower education, and lower levels of civic engagement—even controlling for public access.

In contrast to attitudes, who has actually used the Internet to find information about politics and government? The dependent variable for this model consists of an index ranging from 0 to 3, created from three questions: Have you searched for political information online? Have you looked up information on government services online? Have you seen an online political ad?[66] Again we find that the young, better-educated, and affluent, males, and voters are more likely to be currently engaged in online political activities. There was no difference between Democrats, Republicans, and independents in present use, suggesting that none of these groups would benefit from online voting and registration in the near term. Our multivariate analysis confirms (and extends) the Pew e-government findings that were based on descriptive statistics. In sum, individuals with lower incomes and education and those currently not civically engaged are the least likely to use e-government or participate in politics online, paralleling inequalities in traditional participation.

Analysis of our survey responses on voting in the 2000 elections allows us to compare current participation, as reported by our sample, with interest in digital democracy.[67] Our analysis of voting in the 2000 election agrees with other research on voting. It indicates the poor are significantly less likely to vote, while the educated and elderly are more likely to participate. Those with a political orientation (Republicans and Democrats) are more likely than independents to vote, and females more likely than males. Race and ethnicity also matter: African Americans are more likely than whites to participate, and Asian Americans less likely than whites to do so.

What, then, are the likely consequences of moving political participation onto the Internet? In short, our data on willingness to use information technology for political purposes reveal an online democratic divide—individuals with higher education and income are more supportive of digital democracy, and are more likely to participate in politics online, than the poor and those with lower education. In contrast to Alvarez and Nagler's study of turnout in the Arizona primary, we do not find that race is significant for attitudes about most online participation, controlling for other factors.[68] The exception was Latino attitudes about e-government, which were less favorable than those of whites. African Americans are currently more likely to vote than whites, controlling for education, age, and income. This is not true of support for Internet voting and other forms of online participation. The statistical analysis shows an absence of racial factors affecting attitudes about online participation.

Attitudes toward digital democracy are influenced by gender, partisanship, and age. Women are more hesitant about many political uses of the Internet, but the differences are relatively small. The partisan impact is unclear. Democrats are more supportive of online registration and voting and e-government, but Republicans are more supportive than Democrats if these activities occur in a public setting. More important, there are no significant partisan differences in use of the Internet for political purposes. The young, however, are clearly more interested in online participation and may become more involved in politics if online voting and registration are implemented.

On the down side, the data provide compelling evidence for those who argue that online politics will mirror, or exacerbate, existing disparities in the composition of the electorate based on socioeconomic status. On a positive note, the fact that younger respondents are more supportive of digital democracy suggests the potential for expanding the electorate to include a group that has been traditionally underrepresented. For the young, digital democracy and government may increase their civic engagement because of its convenience and their comfort with new technology. The importance of age in our findings is consistent with previous research on the Arizona Internet voting primary.[69]

Dilemmas for political participation online largely mimic the problem of traditional political participation—those who are better educated are more interested and more able to participate. This indicates that addressing the democratic divide requires more than a technical solution, but attention to educational disparities as well.

Surveys provide one method of predicting the future path of online democracy. Our case study of a local experiment with an online town meeting allows us to probe other issues regarding both digital democracy and e-government and to connect them to our survey findings. We are interested in finding out who participated in the online town meeting and whether digital democracy holds promise for expanding participation. Talking to public officials about various uses of the Internet also allows us to put some aspects of e-government into perspective.

Berkeley, California's, Online Experiment

Berkeley, California, is a community at the cutting edge of experimentation with "e-democracy." Berkeley is a natural incubator for ideas joining e-government with citizen participation. In the shadow of Silicon Valley, the city is able to draw upon a regional culture of digital innovation and a "wired" population of University of California students and academics. The city has a long tradition of political participation harking back to the early 1960s and the Free Speech movement on the Berkeley campus. Although many of the issues have changed, that tradition survives at the local level in public hearings and other city meetings that often attract forty or fifty people from a city of just over 100,000 residents. City officials cite problems with public hearings that straggle on past midnight because so many citizens are waiting their turn to be heard.[70] Berkeley is the type of city where digital-divide issues are likely to emerge, for it shelters low-income, as well as upscale, neighborhoods on its quiet, tree-lined streets. The city also boasts a kaleidoscope of races and cultures: about half of its residents are white, more than 16 percent are Asian American, almost 14 percent are African American, nearly 10 percent are Latino, and approximately 10 percent are from other races or are multiracial.[71] Innovation, participation, and diversity make Berkeley a good test site for learning about e-democracy and the impact of the digital divide for online political participation.

Berkeley residents had the opportunity to register online their opinions about revisions to the city's general plan during the year 2000. The city cooperated with a nonprofit group called Moveon.org, which developed a software program called ActionForum, and used the Berkeley general plan as its first trial.[72] Because of the legal issues entangled in sponsoring an official online forum, the city did not host the forum itself.[73] Berkeley is technically an example of digital democracy rather than e-government, because the city did not sponsor the online town meeting; however, the city gave its blessing to the group, announcing the effort in a press release and brochure.

The ActionForum website displayed a copy of the general plan and allowed citizens to make comments that listed their real names, city of residence, and occupation. The software included a feature that allows other site visitors to agree or disagree with comments and rank them in terms of their importance. Highly ranked comments rise to the top of the list, and lower-ranked comments drop to the bottom. Individuals who read or rate comments remain anonymous, in contrast to those who post their thoughts.[74]

In the assessment of both the city and Moveon.org, the response to the website was limited but nevertheless useful for highlighting some aspects that could be improved in the future, as well as some thorny issues that face such an enterprise. The archived files show thirty-three individuals who participated, but this number included the software developers and their friends. Most of those who participated, according to Moveon.org, were Berkeley activists, so the website did not succeed in enlarging the circle of participation. It did, however, attract some attention beyond those who posted comments. According to Berkeley's communications manager, city employees found it useful to review the comments, and seventy-eight people who were not city employees looked at the site. The forum went online in February 2000, and Moveon.org submitted the final results to the city in August. Citizen input was not effective in shaping the final policy outcomes in this case, because the planning commission decided to scrap the staff's draft of the general plan and develop their own. The Action-Forum was based on the staff version of the proposed revisions.

Limited participation resulted at least partly from the experimental nature of the endeavor. The city did not actively promote the initiative, because it was an initial pilot and there were many questions about how to implement it. The general plan was also a complex document, about 170 pages long, covering more than 600 different policies. As the communications manager suggested, those who did not traditionally participate would have found this a "daunting" first step. It is difficult to know whether issues of technology access and skill made a difference in the Berkeley project, but access was provided at twelve public libraries in the city. City officials were concerned about other aspects of disenfranchisement as well, including the problems of working parents and others who were unable to attend all-night meetings.

The quality of civic discussion is a concern for online forums, as well as the quantity of participation. The prevalence of "junk" on e-democracy websites presented a problem that the creators of the ActionForum attempted to solve with their system for rating comments. One possible difficulty, however, is that judgments may simply reflect the popularity of the opinion rather than its thoughtfulness. The software developers were pleased that none of the comments on the general plan qualified as junk, in their assessment, but more extensive use of the software is needed to conclude that the rating system encourages more civil and considered discussion.

Despite the limited participation in the online forum, the Internet has influenced communication between citizens and government officials in Berkeley other ways. The general plan manager commented on the burgeoning use of e-mail to communicate with officials. The speed, ease, and informality of e-mail encourage people to weigh in with their concerns. Getting this input from citizens has made the plan manager's job "more fun, and less bureaucratic." The communications manager noted that posting documents and other information online required "a transition from bureaucratic speak to a more conversational tone on the Internet." The effort to move government processes onto the web and to make them more transparent has forced a reexamination of how government operates. "The software or being online is not really the crux of the issue," said the city's technology manager. "The crux of the issue is looking at how we do things internally, [and whether] our procedures help or hinder civic engagement."

Although digital democracy, even in Berkeley, has had limited impact, e-government is incrementally changing some of the relationships between citizens and government. The Berkeley initiative demonstrated that holding such a forum is technically feasible and that nongovernmental organizations may have an important role in facilitating such discussions. But the reality is far from the ideal espoused by advocates of participatory democracy. The Berkeley experiment was limited for some reasons that may not apply to other efforts. Yet legal issues, the tenor of public discussion, and the lack of interest expressed by less-educated and low-income individuals in our survey indicate more general potential barriers to widespread use and effective participation.

Participation in the online forum was dominated by a select group of political activists, mirroring traditional participation in city council meetings. These findings are consistent with those of Davis, who argues, "The Internet will not lead to the social and political revolution so widely predicted. . . . Internet users will continue to be the affluent, the already politically interested and active."[75] Although we take a more optimistic position and applaud governments for innovative attempts to increase dialogue with citizens using information technology, the case study suggests some limitations in the potential for expanding participation in government online.

Conclusion

Technology promises to have an increased impact on the way in which individuals interact with government and participate in politics. Online voting and voter registration may be a reality in a number of states by the 2004 presidential elections.[76] In the first binding test of online voting, Arizona Democrats decided in 2000 to elect national convention delegates through Internet voting. In theory, the Internet may provide a means of updating the election system for an information-based society. Access to online political news may also enhance information about candidates and elections, stimulating increased citizen participation.[77]

Our findings on attitudes about digital democracy reveal a contradiction between theory and practice. Many Americans are hesitant about the use of the Internet for purposes such as voting, and others are clearly less interested in online political participation than in uses such as job search and taking courses online. Although e-government delivery of information and services is popular, Berkeley's experiment with an online political forum indicates that there are many hurdles for participatory uses of the Internet, in contrast to the largely informational uses of e-government.

Consistent with cross-national accounts of the digital divide, our survey data reveal an online democratic divide—individuals with higher education and income are more supportive of digital democracy and e-government, and are more likely to participate in politics online, than are the poor and those with lower education.[78] The reasons are not entirely clear. Individuals with limited educational backgrounds may not have the necessary skills or confidence to go online, or they may simply have negative or apathetic attitudes toward politics and government.[79] According to our survey results, the willingness of individuals to use technology for political participation in its various forms is low (with the exception of e-government) in comparison with use of the Internet for economic advancement. The analysis provides evidence that online politics will mirror, or even exacerbate, existing patterns of unequal political participation based on income and education. Representation of racial and ethnic minorities in online politics is unclear. At present, African Americans are more likely to vote than similarly situated whites, but they are no more likely than whites to express interest in online participation, controlling for factors such as income and education.

On the other hand, the young emerge as a group not only more likely to have access to the Internet and computers, but that is also significantly more supportive of digital democracy and e-government. Information technology may increase civic engagement among the young, altering and perhaps expanding the electorate over time. Our prediction of the impact of digital democracy on the representation of the American electorate is therefore mixed. The Internet will neither serve to replicate politics as usual nor transform governance and restore levels of mass political participation. Although the Internet promises to have some positive effects, it will not erase, and may even underscore, the bias of limited participation and representation in American politics that E. E. Schattschneider decried decades ago: "The flaw in the pluralist heaven is that the heavenly chorus sings with a strong upper class accent."[80]

Education emerged as the most important factor in the democratic divide. Support for online voting and online registration were 19 and 22 percentage points higher among individuals with a college degree compared to those with only a high school diploma. This suggests that, in order to close the democratic divide in cyberspace, as well as traditional politics, education will be crucial as well as access to technology. More than 200 years ago, Thomas Jefferson argued that public education was necessary for an educated citizenry and for the health of the republic. In the future, attention to information literacy and access may be mechanisms for achieving equal opportunity in the political sphere, but participation will also be rooted in factors that have traditionally been associated with civic engagement.

Notes

1. Putnam 2000.
2. Abramson 1983; Campbell et al. 1960; Conway 1991; Wolfinger and

Rosenstone 1980; Rosenstone and Hansen 1993; Piven and Cloward 1988; Verba and Nie 1972; Verba, Schlozman, and Brady 1995.

3. Smith 1989.

4. Bimber 2001; Norris 2001; Alvarez and Nagler 2002; Shah, Kwak, and Holbert 2001; Scheufele and Shah 2000; Solop 2000; Tolbert and McNeal 2003.

5. Davis 1999.

6. Campbell et al. 1960; Wolfinger and Rosenstone 1980.

7. Norris 1999; Rosenthal 1997; Dionne 1996; Baldassare 2000, chap. 2.

8. Peters 1996, chap. 3.

9. Pateman 1970.

10. On "discursive democracy," see Dryzek 1990; on "strong democracy," see Barber 1984; on "teledemocracy," see Toffler 1995; on "deliberative democracy," see Fishkin 1993; on general participatory models, see Peters 1996.

11. Budge 1996.

12. Dryzek 1990; Barber 1984.

13. Butler and Ranney 1994; Bowler, Donovan, and Tolbert 1998; Bowler and Donovan 1998; Gerber 1999; Magleby 1984; Mendolsohn and Parkin 2001.

14. Norris 2001, 96; Toffler 1995.

15. For a more general discussion, see Norris 2001, 97–98 and 95–111.

16. Rheingold 1993; Budge 1996; Hague and Loader 1999; Grossman 1995.

17. Initiative and Referenda Institute 2002.

18. Gibson 2002; Alvarez and Nagler 2002.

19. Alvarez and Nagler 2002; Wilhelm 2000; Margolis and Resnick 2000; Putnam 2000, 166–80. According to critics, there are other drawbacks to online politics as well. For example, some argue that the Internet will narrow the focus of attention by fostering selective exposure to political information consistent with individual preferences and interests. Reduced exposure to conflicting views may reduce citizen political tolerance (Sunstein 2001).

20. Wolfinger and Rosenstone 1980.

21. Norris 2001, 98; Putnam 2000, 174–75. See also Davis and Owen 1998; Davis 1999; McChesney 1999; Wilhelm 2000.

22. Bimber 2001.

23. Tolbert and McNeal 2003.

24. Weber and Bergman 2001.

25. Shah, Kwak, and Holbert 2001.

26. Rosenstone and Hansen 1993; Verba, Schlozman, and Brady 1995.

27. Bimber 1999.

28. Gibson 2002.

29. Solop 2000.

30. Alvarez and Nagler 2002.

31. King 1997.

32. Multivariate regression analysis suggests elderly, nonwhite, unemployed and rural residents were also statistically less likely to engage in Internet voting, controlling for other factors (Alvarez and Nagler 2002).

33. With only fifteen counties in the state of Arizona, the estimates of minority and white voters are so aggregated that they may not be representative of actual statewide voting patterns. Such a small number of cases violates one of the assumptions of multiple regression. The central limit theorem requires that there be a minimum of fifty cases in order for the dependent variable to be normally distributed. With such a small number of cases, the research runs the risk of incorrect inferences.

34. Clift 2000.

35. Markle Foundation 1999; Norris, Fletcher, and Holden 2001.

36. West 2000, 2. See also Chadwick 2001; Clift 2000; Norris 2001; Tapscott 1997.

37. Chadwick 2001. See www.firstgov.gov.

38. See Stowers 1999 and Norris, Fletcher, and Holden 2001.

39. Seifert and Petersen 2002; Stowers 1999.

40. Fountain 2001, 6; Seifert and Petersen 2002.

41. West 2001.

42. Gartner Group 2000.

43. Chadwick 2001; Fountain 2001, 4; West, forthcoming; but on e-government at the local level, see Ho 2002.

44. National Performance Review 1993; for similar arguments about reinventing government, see Osborne and Gaebler 1992.

45. Seifert and Petersen 2002.

46. Layne and Lee (2001) delineate a four-stage model of e-government evolution (cataloging, transaction, vertical integration, and horizontal integration). The availability of transactions on the web represents advancement to at least the second stage of implementation. Others define the evolution of e-government by the four stages of presence, interaction, transaction, and

transformation. While an example of "presence" is a basic website that lists cursory information about an agency, hours of operation, mailing address, or phone numbers but has no interactive capabilities, "interactive" web-based initiatives offer enhanced capabilities, including instructions for obtaining services or downloadable forms to be printed and mailed back to an agency. "Transaction" allows clients to complete entire tasks electronically through self-service operations such as license renewals, paying taxes and fees, and submitting bids for procurement contracts. Transformation is the highest order of evolution for e-government initiatives, including robust customer relationship management capabilities required to handle a full range of questions, problems and needs (Seifert and Peterson 2002). Although there are currently few examples of this type of initiative, some suggest that, at its most advanced level, e-government could potentially reorganize, combine, and or eliminate existing government agencies and replace them with virtual ones.

47. West, forthcoming.

48. Stowers 1999.

49. Fagan and Fagan 2001; Fountain 2001, 21–22; Stowers 1999.

50. Norris 2001, 128. See also Clift 2000; Melitski 2001; Tapscott 1997.

51. West, forthcoming; Clift 2000.

52. West, forthcoming.

53. Seifert and Petersen 2002.

54. See West 2000.

55. McNeal et al. 2003.

56. Kettl 2000.

57. West 2001; Chadwick 2001; McNeal et al. 2003.

58. Pew Internet and American Life Project 2002.

59. West 2001; Pew Internet and American Life Project 2002. The public opinion poll reported in West (2001) also shows that men are more likely than women to have used e-government. The poll cited by West is the Hart-Teeter for the Council for Excellence in Government national survey taken in August 2000.

60. Pew Internet and American Life Project 2002; West 2001.

61. Because the dependent variables are binary, logistic regression was used to analyze the data. See table A5.1 for the results.

62. See Bimber 1999.

63. The result showing that Asian Americans are less likely than whites to support e-government is statistically significant at .10, which is borderline. The sample for Asian Americans was also small, so we do not have sufficient

confidence in the results for Asian Americans to report them as significant findings.

64. See King, Tomz, and Wittenberg 2000. We calculate the change in the probability of access and support for online participation caused by moving from a variable's high to low value while simultaneously keeping all other variables set to their mean (or 0 or 1 category for dichotomous variables). The change in the probability of support for online participation caused by moving from low to high values of the independent variables allows for effective substantive comparisons across independent variables.

65. Table A5.2 shows the results of a multivariate regression using combined scales for attitudes about online political participation, attitudes about online participation in a public place, and actual experience with online participation. Since the dependent variables are measured on an ordinal scale, our estimates are based on ordered logistic regression.

66. See the last column in table A5.2 for the results of the multivariate regression analysis.

67. We created a dummy variable for the 2000 elections, coding responses as 1 for voting and 0 for not voting.

68. Alvarez and Nagler 2002.

69. Solop 2000.

70. Both city officials and community activists noted this problem of a participatory bottleneck.

71. U.S. Census Bureau 2000.

72. The software developers involved in Moveon.org and the ActionForum are Berkeley residents and creators of the Broederbon Software "flying toaster" screensaver and the popular computer quiz game "You Don't Know Jack."

73. The collaboration between the city and Moveon.org was beneficial to both parties. Organizations outside city government have more discretion in monitoring a website for slanderous content or in controlling content through ranking or other methods. (First amendment issues prevent city governments from censoring material in any way.) Moveon.org valued the feedback it received from the city, and the city saw this as an important experiment with a new venue for participation. The first amendment issue is likely to have a broader influence in the implementation of officially sponsored online forums. Other legal issues specific to California hampered the exchange between officials and citizens through the forum. The city attorney's office ruled that council members and members of commissions were not allowed to participate in the online forum, based on California state law

called the "Brown Act" that prohibits elected officials from gathering to discuss issues or make decisions outside of public meetings.

74. For a demonstration and the archived comments from the Berkeley general plan, go to www.actionforum.com.

75. Davis 1999.

76. Brookings Institution 2000.

77. Tolbert and McNeal 2003.

78. Norris 2001.

79. James 2001.

80. Schattschneider 1960, 34–35.

Chapter 6

Beyond the Divides: Toward Opportunity and Equity

with Lisa Dotterweich

O ur analysis has allowed us to achieve several goals: to move beyond a narrow definition of the "digital divide," to better describe patterns of access and skill, and to describe and predict the impacts of these disparities for economic opportunity and democratic participation. We accomplished this by expanding the definition of the problem so it includes the range of public policy concerns on the issue and by gathering data on skills, attitudes, and experiences relevant to these concerns. We have provided more accurate evidence than existing studies have done, through a large sample of low-income and minority respondents and the use of statistical controls. In short, we have presented a number of arguments about the ways in which the policy "map" of the digital divide must be altered to more closely resemble the reality of information technology-related disparities. In this chapter, we briefly trace the new geography of the divides and their policy significance. We then highlight patterns that cut across the four divides and discuss current and future public policy.

Measuring the Access Divide

Despite arguments to the contrary made by policymakers and scholars, the access divide that appeared during the 1990s persists. The evidence has sometimes been muddled by weak research methods and unsophisticated analyses. The debate has been confused by a number of claims that we hope to lay to rest.

First, it is erroneous to allege that the access divide is dead. Enduring, and statistically significant, gaps remain in terms of income, race, ethnicity, education, and age, even as more Americans join the ranks of those online. These differences appeared in our analysis of Internet access since the mid-1990s, and they still matter today for Internet access, e-mail addresses, and computer ownership. The gender gap has been more transient, but we cannot make the assumption that the other disparities are vanishing as well. The momentum gathering behind diffusion does not erase all differences.

Second, some studies have suggested that race and ethnicity do not affect the access divide. Our data, with its large sample of minorities, demonstrate that African Americans and Latinos have significantly lower rates of home computer ownership, e-mail use, and Internet access than whites, even when we control for differences in age, education, and income.

Factors such as education, income, and age, however, influence access to an even greater extent than race and ethnicity. The survey data we examined from 1996 onward showed that income played a more complex role in the early days of the Internet but that better-educated and younger individuals have been enthusiastic users throughout. This suggests an array of factors are involved in the access divide—the affordability of technology, knowledge of technology and the skill to use it, and exposure to, and attitudes toward, technology use.

Uncovering the Skills Divide

It is clear that a skills divide also exists and that it closely follows the contours of the access divide. Those who are most likely to need assistance with computers are older, less-educated, low-income, African American, and Latino. Age and education make the greatest difference. Both dimensions of skill—technical competence and information literacy—echoed the same disparities as the access divide.

The existence of a parallel skills divide, while not surprising, has a number of troubling implications. To us, the question of skills transcends the issue of computer ownership and home Internet access, for it is technology skills that most clearly enable individuals to pursue opportunities for economic advancement or political participation, as well as other goals. Nevertheless, more than a fifth of our sample reported needing help with the simplest of all tasks—using a mouse and keyboard—indicating that they were completely devoid of any technical competence. Approximately one-third needed help locating information using computers. This may demonstrate a lack of familiarity with computerized data bases and the Internet, but it could also indicate more serious problems with basic literacy and with navigation through the proliferating sources of information in modern society. Our data cannot address this latter question directly, but it is certainly a topic worth pursuing in further research.

The access and skills divides matter for public policy because of their potential to influence economic opportunity and civic participation. Pronounced inequalities in these areas, of course, already exist. The policy question is whether the use of technology promises to exacerbate or ameliorate current inequities. To explore this question in the areas of economic opportunity and political participation, we measured the possible impact of the access and skills divides through the attitudes of respondents as well as their experiences. We reason that, even where experience is limited, attitudes give us some evidence of the interests and aspirations of our respondents. We can therefore better define the problem—do people lacking access and skills also lack an interest in information technology and its uses? With experimental or rare applications such as Internet voting and electronic town meetings, we can find out how receptive the general public is to such innovations and whether attitudes differ among various groups in the population.

Assessing the Economic Opportunity Divide

Computer use on the job is prevalent and growing and has contributed toward rising skills demands in the work force. We found that just under half of our respondents with a high school education or less reported actually using the computer at work at least once during the past month. About one-quarter of these less-educated workers used the Internet.

Most Americans identify computer skills with economic opportunity, and the poor and less educated are no different. Attitudes about technology and economic opportunity do differ, however, by age, race and ethnicity, employment status, and, to a modest extent, gender. Older respondents are less interested in technology and economic opportunity. African Americans, Latinos, the unemployed, and women, however, seem particularly sensitive to the potential connection between technology and opportunity. This suggests that, in low-income and minority communities, the task is not so much to convince individuals that these skills are necessary, but rather to make technology and instruction available and relevant to job search, career development, and small business needs. Experience with the developing area of online job search supports this contention. African Americans are more likely than whites to have actually used the Internet to search for a job or to take a course online, even though African Americans are statistically less likely to have access. We conclude that, although the access and skills divide may in fact diminish economic opportunities for those who are already disadvantaged, substantial interest in information technology and economic opportunity exists among many disadvantaged groups.

Mapping the Democratic Divide

Technology promises to have an increased impact on the way in which individuals interact with government and participate in politics, as debates over Internet voting and the advent of online registration and absentee voting show. Some scholars predict that minorities and the poor will be disenfranchised by these developments, although the empirical record is based on limited use of these innovations. Our data on attitudes regarding various forms of online participation, therefore, open a unique window to the future, amid competing claims, hype, and confusion over the impact of the Internet in the public sphere.

We found that use of government websites for information about services was more popular among respondents than was use for online political participation. More than three-quarters of Americans were willing to look up government information online, but slightly less than half were willing to vote online or participate in an online town meeting. Support for online voter registration was considerably higher, and support for Internet voting increased 10 percentage points if it occurred in a public place where access and security issues are less relevant. Some partisan differences appeared, with Democrats generally more supportive of online registration and voting but Republicans more supportive of online voting if it occurred in a public place. Our survey results and our case study of an online forum in Berkeley, California, indicate that widespread use of the Internet for voting and town meetings is not on the immediate horizon, but it may be in the future if difficulties such as legal issues and security are resolved.

Attitudes about politics and government online differ among groups, but they promise to reinforce most existing disparities in political participation. Those who are most likely to support use of the Internet for voting, registering, looking up government information, and participating in town meetings are generally those who participate now (the educated and the affluent, and those who voted in the prior election). The major way in which technology augurs change in patterns of political participation is through its potential to mobilize the young. The young were consistently more likely to express interest in online political participation across the range of questions we asked.

The Internet may constitute a double-edged sword for political participation—mobilizing some groups that are currently less likely to participate in politics (the young) while perpetuating or perhaps even magnifying disparities based on education and income. Our findings agree with the well-established body of research on political participation, that lower-income and less-educated individuals are least likely to participate. Race and ethnicity did not matter for most questions about political engagement in our survey (except that Latinos were less supportive of e-government than whites). Traditionally, African Americans are more likely to vote, controlling for income and education, but this did not appear to be true in regard to online voting or other forms of participation.

Across the Four Divides

What is our prognosis for the policy landscape of the future, in light of our assessment of these four divides? We find both barriers and resources for bridging the divides.

The access divide currently presents a gloomy picture, with persistent gaps in home access based on age, income, race, ethnicity, and

WHAT MATTERS

What Matters across the Four Divides

Barriers	Resources
Access	
Disparities by income, education, race, ethnicity, and age	General growth in computer and Internet access; high likelihood of access for young
Skills	
Disparities that mirror access divide; poor and old less interested in learning skills	Generally positive attitudes toward learning and public access, especially among the young and African Americans, sometimes Latinos
Economic Opportunity	
Lack of computer skills, reading, and math for economic mobility and opportunity	Generally positive attitudes about technology for economic advancement; especially among the young and African Americans, sometimes Latinos, women, the unemployed
Democratic Participation	
Continued or increased disparities based on education, income, interest (measured by previous participation)	Positive attitudes among young, who are currently underrepresented

education. The skills divide is mostly ominous as well, for findings on the skills front generally reinforce the findings on access. The access and skills divides seem closely linked, perhaps in a vicious circle—those without skills have little need to use computers, and those without frequent availability have little chance to develop the skills that they need through trial and error and practice. Frequent computer use occurs at home or work, underscoring the relevance of home access for developing acumen. Yet the skills divide is more complex than either the access debates or needs for technical competence suggest. Reading skills and information literacy are needed both to promote further diffusion of information technology and to allow individuals to capture the full benefits of technology. The barriers are more substantial than indicated in previous political discourse on the issue.

There is cause for some optimism, however, in the favorable opinions that most Americans hold regarding technology and their willingness to use it for many purposes. African Americans, in particular, express positive attitudes about public access, learning new skills, and using technology for economic advancement. The results on the democratic divide give rise to both optimism, because of technology's potential to involve younger citizens, and pessimism, because the Internet promises to perpetuate and perhaps widen disparities in political participation currently based on income and education. More generally, how will differences based on age, gender, income, race, ethnicity, and education develop in the near future?

Younger individuals, who have enthusiastically embraced the Internet, will continue to lead the way in information technology use. Disparities in access and skills based on age will disappear over time. Public policy may encourage older individuals to gain new computer skills at work and at public access sites such as libraries and community centers. For the workforce, however, it is those who have a number of years before retirement who are most likely to represent a policy problem, if they lack the skills to enjoy some choice and mobility in the labor market. Training and continuing education are concerns for this segment of the population. Our examination of technology use for political participation suggests that widespread use for voting is somewhat distant. Steps such as training to use newly digitized voting machines, assistance at public access sites, and alternatives such as mail ballots may help to ease the transition toward greater use of technology for voting. Public access may also be helpful in encouraging older individuals to take advantage of information and services available through government websites.

Most gender gaps in access and skills have vanished over the years, and the gender differences that remain primarily involve attitudes toward learning (preferences for more hands-on instruction) or use of technology (less enthusiasm for Internet job search or participation in an online town meeting). This suggests a difference in interests rather than an inability to participate economically or politically. One reason that the gender-based access and skills divides have been temporary, we hypothesize, is that women have similar educational opportunities as men. As computers and the Internet became more widespread, and the range of applications increased, women had the ability to master the new technology. Disparities based on income, race, and ethnicity may prove more persistent, for the quality of education in the United States varies greatly along lines of class and race. Even if we control for educational attainment, our measures tell us little about the content of that education and how well it has prepared individuals to learn new skills and to adapt to social change.

Income was significant for predicting disparities in access and skills, which suggests that access and skills are intertwined. As mentioned above, lower-income individuals may lack the educational experiences necessary to prepare them for technology use, even if we control for educational attainment, and so may be less likely to invest in computers. But the cost of computers and Internet access may also represent a hurdle for low-income households. Even as prices fall, computer purchases compete with other needs, especially for the poorest. As we have seen, frequent computer and Internet use occurs at home or at work, so those without home access may have fewer chances to develop skills.

Low-income respondents were less likely to be interested in using the Internet for e-government and online town meetings, but they were not less supportive of using the Internet for voting or registering to vote. Disinterest in e-government is of particular concern, because, unlike Internet voting or online forums, e-government has been widely adopted by local, state, and federal governments. It is the most popular use of technology in our survey, with even more widespread support than online job search or distance learning. Apathy or negative attitudes about e-government among the poor distinguish them as markedly different from the rest of the population. The potential benefits of e-government, such as greater transparency in government and easier access to public services, will largely bypass the poor. Because low-income people often depend upon public services for their daily needs, this finding is all the more disconcerting.

The poor did not differ from other Americans in their favorable attitudes toward technology as a tool for achieving economic opportunity, and the unemployed were actually more likely than the employed to think that computer skills are needed to get ahead. Disinterest in e-government and online forums may signal disengagement from government rather than apathy toward technology. The problem of limited political participation among the poor predates the Internet, and the answer to this particular problem lies outside of the realm of technology.

Race and ethnicity have been prominent in debates over the digital divide. Our data show that race matters, but in complex and sometimes puzzling ways. Income and education alone are not sufficient to explain the gap between African American and white access and skills. Some commentators have argued that African Americans do not see the content of the Internet as relevant and that there is a cultural divide. Yet African Americans (and, less consistently, Latinos) had more-positive attitudes than whites about public access, learning new skills, and using technology in pursuit of economic opportunity. This means that we need to look elsewhere for explanations. Racial segregation, concentrated poverty, and a lack of exposure to technology within poor African American neighborhoods may have some effect over and above the influence of family income and individual educational attainment in these areas. In low-income minority communities, institutions such as schools and libraries may lack the resources to provide adequate educational preparation, access, and computer training. Personal networks may not include friends and relatives who are themselves "plugged in" and able to provide encouragement and mentoring. We cannot provide direct evidence for these conjectures, or some of the earlier hypotheses about the quality of educational experiences, but they make sense in view of the data.

The positive attitudes expressed by African American respondents also provide some ammunition for those who are worried about racial stereotypes being unintentionally perpetuated by attention to a racial dimension of the access and skills divides. The problem is not that African Americans do not "get" technology. In fact, they hear the message more clearly than most and may be even more motivated to learn when given a chance. Despite lower rates of access and skills, African Americans are more likely than whites to have used the Internet for online job search and distance learning.

Finally, the issue of education looms large across the four divides and, to us, presents the most urgent need for preparing workers and citizens for the information age. The results of national literacy surveys cast doubt on the ability of many Americans to cope with the demands of technology, work, and political participation. Education already influences economic advancement and political participation, apart from the issue of information technology. With the advent of the Internet, basic skills such as reading, the ability to locate information, to use it to solve problems, and to evaluate its appropriateness are all necessary to use information technology to its full potential. Similar skills have been identified more generally as workplace competencies in the new economy, and the Internet raises the literacy bar for political participation to some extent. The significance of education is clear if we examine who has the most experience using (and is presumably most able to use) the Internet in a variety of ways.

Digital Experience and Education: Evidence from the Survey

As another way of summarizing the results of the survey, we created an index of seven questions regarding applications of technology to measure what we call "digital experience" in key areas: whether an individual (1) can locate information on the web, (2) has searched for political information online, (3) has looked up information on government services online, (4) has searched for or applied for a job online, (5) has taken a class online, (6) has used the computer to do homework, and (7) has used the computer to find books in the library without assistance. Together, these responses not only measure experience with information technology, but also imply the ability to use technology to gather information and perform complex tasks. Positive responses to each question were coded 1 (0 for negative responses), and then the seven questions were summed to create an index ranging from 0 to 7.

A frequency graph (histogram, shown in figure 6.1) of the digital experience index reveals a relatively bell-shaped curve, which would be expected with a "normal" distribution, where the majority of people fall around the average. The curve is somewhat skewed, however, at the lower end. The spike at the far left shows that a number of respondents scored 0, having no experience in using information technology for any of these purposes. The fact that these respondents were not able to even locate information on the Internet suggests that many of these individuals lack rudimentary skills as well as experience. The mean score was 3.1, indicating that the average respondent in the survey answered positively to three of the seven questions. About 37 percent of respondents could be classified

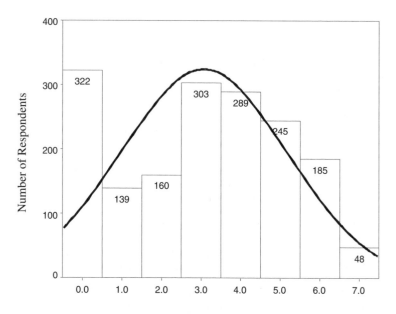

Proficiency—Number of Tasks Respondent Can Complete

Note: Responses to seven questions were used to create the index of digital experience, which approximates a normal distribution. Each column represents the number of survey respondents who could complete that number of online tasks. The graph is slightly skewed to the left, reflecting the low-income sample.

Figure 6.1   Distribution of Digital Experience in the United States

as having low digital experience, with scores ranging from 0 to 2 on the index. At the same time, 28 percent could be defined as highly experienced, with scores ranging from 5 to 7 on the index. Thirty-five percent had moderate experience, with scores of 3 or 4.

What factors explain varying levels of digital experience among survey respondents? Using the index as the dependent variable, or the result to be explained, we examined the influence of the demographic factors used throughout the book as well as several measures of access to information technology: computer ownership, an e-mail address, and home access to the Internet.[1] Our analysis reveals that digital experience was related to home Internet access and e-mail access (but not computer ownership). Apparently home Internet access is more conducive to digital experience than access that is limited to either work or public access venues. When controlling for access, digital experience, however, is not significantly related to race, ethnicity, or income, but it is clearly linked to education. Digital experience is to some extent a result of interest in the particular activities we included in the index as well. Men, the young, the employed, and the educated have more digital experience, consistent with the patterns of interest in online politics, job search, and distance learning found in earlier chapters.

The policy issues that emerge, then, are access, skills, and education. What resources currently exist for closing the access and skills gaps? Where do our data lead us in terms of policy recommendations?

The Current Environment

A number of government and nonprofit initiatives attempt to broaden access to technology. By one recent count, more than 20,000 programs exist.[2] This flurry of activity to some extent conceals the small scale and tenuous existence of many of these efforts, their patchwork coverage of poor communities, and a lack of research on the effectiveness of existing programs. Nevertheless, some progress has been made in terms of providing more hardware in schools and libraries. The challenge for the future will be to maintain and expand these resources and to use them effectively to develop skills and to meet the needs of the communities they serve.

The major programs currently in place address public access in schools, libraries, and community technology centers (CTCs) rather than home access. Government activity in this area is primarily federal, although at least six states have passed legislation to either fund infrastructure or study the issue.[3] The largest federal effort is the E-Rate program, which expended over $2.25 billion in fiscal year 2001. This is a modest expenditure, however, in a $3.5 trillion federal budget and less than the $2.5 billion the Navy will be spending for just two LPD-17 amphibious ships by 2003.[4] The E-Rate was established through the Telecommunications Act of 1996 (PL 104-104), and it offers considerable discounts on telecommunications technologies to libraries and schools (ranging from 20 percent to 90 percent). The depth of the discount is calculated on the basis of economic need, with some additional priority given to rural locations. In the first two years of its operation, E-Rate benefited nearly 80,000 schools and libraries. The lion's share of the funds—84 percent—went to public schools. The program has apparently targeted poor communities, as intended. The E-Rate program, however, has limited purposes, funding wiring, phone and Internet access, rather than computer equipment, staff support, or staff training.[5]

The other two main federal programs provide a broader range of services, but to fewer beneficiaries. The Technologies Opportunities Program (TOP) awards matching grants for model projects that exhibit innovative use of technology. TOP addresses issues involved in the access and skills divides, but is stretched across a variety of objectives, including meeting the technology needs of government agencies. CTCs provide access to technology, training, and sometimes other services, such as job search, after-school enrichment, and adult and continuing education.[6] Programs may be located in libraries, churches, public housing, the facilities of community-based organizations, or a variety of places in low-income urban and rural areas. Nearly 400 centers have been funded, but like the TOP program, the thrust of the CTC program is to support model projects over the short-term rather than to provide a comprehensive or sustained solution. Together, the TOP and CTC programs totaled about $110 million in fiscal year 2001. The Bush administration has attempted to eliminate both programs.

Resistance from civil rights groups and congressional support have stalled such cuts. Pressure to continue a federal role in the promotion of technology use has come from sources closer to the administration as well. The President's Council of Advisors on Science and Technology identified the extensive diffusion of broadband technology as potentially contributing $500 billion annually to gross domestic product over the next ten years. In response, some technology industry representatives have called for government support of broadband in underserved areas. Apparently such arguments have been difficult to ignore entirely, although the White House has not proposed any specific policy. Despite the administration's stance on the CTC and TOP programs, President Bush declared in August 2002 that bringing "the promise of broadband technology to millions of Americans" was needed "to make sure the economy grows" and to "stay on the cutting edge of innovation."[7]

Some private giving has also helped to extend technology access. The Bill and Melinda Gates Foundation committed more than $250 million in equipment, and the foundation also trains library staff in the latest technology. A score of other foundations have some involvement in the issue: Annie E. Casey, Kellogg, the National Cristina Foundation, and corporate foundations such as AOL/Time Warner, AT&T, Microsoft Giving, BellSouth, Cisco, IBM, Marco-Polo, and SBC. The Boys and Girls Clubs of America, the Girl Scouts of America, and the National Urban League have digital divide initiatives. This interest on the part of many donors and volunteer organizations offers important resources, but efforts are fragmented and do not necessarily replace a steady commitment of government support.

Some increased public access is evident, as a result of federal, state, local, and private spending. According to the American Library Association, 95 percent of public libraries now offer Internet access to the public, in comparison to 1998, when 76 percent of libraries offered the service. Nearly half of public libraries in the U.S. provide some training for patrons in computer use or the evaluation of information on the web.[8]

Few data exist, though, on how well the supply of hardware, software, and assistance matches the demand from library patrons, especially in poor communities. Public access sites may require users to wait long periods for their turn, impose strict time limits on computer sessions, filter out useful websites deemed to have controversial content, and provide users with little privacy. Libraries in poor urban neighborhoods or rural areas may have only a few terminals and insufficient numbers of staff to help patrons or to provide more systematic training. Computer users at a library or a community center also may not have time and leisure to explore and use the computer in the same way that someone with an Internet connection at home would. In many communities, access through CTCs or nonprofit programs is sporadic or nonexistent.[9]

The greatest effort on the part of federal, state, and local governments in closing the access and skills divide has been in providing computers and Internet connectivity in the schools. Schools in low-income communities now have 5.3 students per computer in comparison to the national average of 4.9 students per computer.[10] Most schools are now wired for the Internet, as a result of the E-Rate program.[11] Still, there are some significant holes in school access and substantial inequality in the use of technology. Schools with a high concentration of African American students have less computer access than other poor schools, although that gap seems to be narrowing.[12] Simple ratios also obscure differences in the quality and use of equipment. Anecdotal reports paint a grim portrait. Financially strapped districts often scrape by with aging and outdated technology. Schools in low-income areas often lack the technical support staff and teacher training needed to integrate technology throughout the curriculum, so students get little practice in the varied ways in which they might apply technology and even less experience searching for or critically evaluating information on the web. Several studies have shown that lower-achieving students enjoy less frequent use of computers during the school day and have more experience using computers for remedial drills rather than exploring the Internet for assignments. This tendency may be even more pronounced in poor urban schools. Teachers in such schools may have less experience using technology. Computer use can also absorb precious class time for instructing students who lack basic computer skills, and fewer students have home computers or Internet access to complete assignments later.[13]

Public Policy for the Future

Despite tangible progress toward closing technology gaps, more needs to be done. Technology in K–12 schools is an important part of the solution, for what happens in schools today will determine the dimensions of the access and skills divides in the future. Our data, however, describe the experiences and attitudes of adults twenty-one years of age and older. No matter what advances are made in improving access and skills within public school systems, significant challenges will persist for adults who have not acquired important technical and information skills—and who will remain within the workforce, the community, and the electorate for many years to come.

The primary argument against government action on this issue is that the market is effectively closing the access gap and that public intervention is a waste of public dollars or unwarranted distortion of market forces. Both Adam Thierer, of the conservative think tank the Heritage Foundation, and Benjamin Compaine, the editor of a volume of essays on the digital divide, contend that this is the case. They point to the rapid diffusion of the Internet and falling prices of computers and Internet access services.[14] Compaine also argues that digital technology is becoming easier to use, reducing skills barriers as well as cost.[15] Thierer's critique is loaded with rhetoric about big government, competition and choice in the free market, and the possibility that government subsidies will entail more government regulation of the technology industry. Although Compaine shares many of Thierer's concerns—for example, that subsidies may lock in less efficient and more expensive technologies—he concedes that government has facilitated the diffusion of some technological advances in the past and that there may be some role to be played by government in this case. Cross-subsidies for universal access assisted in the diffusion of the telephone, just as federal highway support subsidized the use of automobiles. Compaine argues that the proper role of government is less than clear in the case of information technology, though, and that it is advisable to wait to find out how necessary computers will be in the future and whether the market will close the gap on its own.[16]

We disagree with Thierer and Compaine on several fronts. First, the preceding chapters demonstrate that information technology use has current and potential benefits for society and that technology access and skills are public goods that have spillover benefits beyond the individuals concerned. Disparities in information technology merit not just continued, but greater, policy attention. The social costs of ignoring technology disparities are two-fold: failure to fully realize the potential offered by technology and deepening inequalities in economic opportunity and democratic citizenship.

Productivity gains during the late 1990s resulted from the use of technology in a broad range of industries and uses. Widespread technical skills and information literacy are important resources for increasing efficiency and innovation throughout the economy. Geographic inequality in the distribution of technology skills may also restrict the ability of communities to compete for business investment, particularly for industries requiring a skilled workforce.

For individuals, deficient technology skills and limited education constrain the possibilities for economic mobility. Continued technological diffusion and change portend a future where even more jobs will depend upon information technology use. Although jobs requiring few or no computer skills will continue to be available, many of them will offer low wages and few benefits. Americans clearly recognize this new reality in the labor market, as our survey shows, and women, racial and ethnic minorities, and the unemployed are even more likely than others to believe that a level playing field requires computer skills.

Prevalent skills and access are also needed if society is to capitalize on technology's potential to make political information and opportunities for participation more accessible. Currently, the use of technology is most developed as a means of communicating political information rather than as a mechanism for direct participation through voting or community forums. The proliferation of political and government websites, however, represents an important step toward enhancing civic engagement by increasing information access. Furthermore, information technology may yet provide a means of slowing or reversing declining levels of political participation, by making acts such as voting or commenting on community issues easier for many. The interest of the young in technology may have a generational effect, raising levels of participation in the long term. These are important potential benefits for society.

At the same time, both attitudes toward online participation and evidence regarding access and skills show that the hurdles for political participation may be increased for the less educated and the poor. Because African Americans and Latinos disproportionately fill the ranks of the poor and less educated, the overall effect may well be to diminish the political participation of minorities as well. The principle of political equality demands that we must not leave whole segments of the population unable to participate as the use of technology evolves.

Second, both Thierer and Compaine wrongly focus the question on access alone. Inexpensive computers, discount Internet providers, WebTV, and the used computer market may fill some of the current gap in access, but our data demonstrate that affordability is not the only problem. Compaine's contention that skills requirements are negligible is also clearly incorrect. Demands for technical competence are indeed lower than in past decades—PC users no longer need to know programming languages such as Fortran. The Internet, however, has emphasized the need for literacy and information skills as well as technical competence. One study of CTCs, for example, documented the problems that individuals with low literacy skills had in understanding content on the Internet.[17] The market is not likely to resolve this problem, which affects economic opportunities and political participation as well. There is an important public role in supporting the acquisition of information literacy, as well as technical competence, in order to capture the social benefits of technology and promote equal chances for political and economic participation. What more, then, needs to be done?

On the basis of our survey and our review of the social significance of information technology, we put forward a few general recommendations.

1. *Attention to skills development in public access sites.* One contribution that we hope to make through this study is to focus more attention on the skills needed for technical competence and information literacy. The data in our survey demonstrate that more than one-fifth of the population lacks even the most basic technical skills (the ability to use a mouse and keyboard) and that a third of the population needs help finding information using the Internet and data bases. Public policy should not only encourage public access, but also provide more systematic training and assistance in public places such as libraries, community centers, and public schools after hours. Printed manuals and online assistance are less accessible to inexperienced users and less-educated individuals, and our survey showed that hands-on personal assistance and group instruction were the most widely preferred methods of help. We found that respondents who already had a computer or Internet access at home were as likely to use public access at libraries as individuals without home access. This indicates that public access sites are more than places to boot up and log on—that the availability of assistance attracts users as well. This is an important role that can likely be improved upon in the future.

CTCs and public institutions such as libraries and schools (particularly adult education programs) can provide assistance with distance education and locating information on jobs or government services as well as providing technical support and general assistance in navigating the web. Public and nonprofit institutions have a role to play in exploiting the "public goods" nature of the technology and the advantages that accrue to society in terms of workforce development and community participation.

For these reasons, we see public access as an important element in any strategy to address the access and skills divides. Our data, however, leave us with nagging questions about the current effectiveness of public access. Low rates of use are problematic. Only 13 percent of those without a home computer, and only 9 percent without home Internet access, use computers or the Internet at a library. Those without computers and the Internet are not more likely to use public access than those who do have home access. This is true, even though most respondents say in the abstract that they are willing to use public access and that they overwhelmingly favor schools and libraries as access venues. These are currently the most common places for public use. Poor and minority respondents are more likely than others to have positive images of libraries as community gathering places, indicating that the setting itself is not an issue. More needs to be known about the actual facilities and services available in public access venues, especially in poor communities.

There are also inherent limitations to public access as the sole venue for computer use. The ideal situation is broader home access to computers and the Internet, as well as continued public access for the development of skills, information about Internet uses and software, and increased availability of more expensive options such as broadband.

2. *Limited experimentation with an educational technology subsidy.* Most government and nonprofit programs currently support public access rather than increased home computer and Internet access. Some nonprofit programs offer low-income participants special discounts, loans, or refurbished equipment, but the scale of these initiatives is small in comparison to public access programs. Should public dollars provide subsidies for low-income families, such as vouchers?

Some proponents have raised this idea—for example, a group of Silicon Valley executives, including the chief executive of Novell, Eric Schmidt. The proposal fielded by this group, called ClickStart, featured a federal voucher that would cover both computer hardware and Internet access. Eligible individuals would pay $5 dollars a month and get a $10 monthly voucher that would be honored by participating vendors.[18] Some other proposals have been put forward, for example, for a flat $500 federal voucher.[19]

Survey data: Opinions on vouchers. We asked our survey respondents for their opinion on vouchers. Our survey included questions on support for government programs to provide computers to low-income families and government programs to provide Internet access to low-income families and rural residents.[20] When the question was posed in this general way, a slight majority of respondents was in favor of such government intervention. About 56 percent of respondents supported government funding for computers for low-income households, and 52 percent supported a government program to subsidize Internet access. This indicates a fair amount of support for a policy such as vouchers, although the specific details—the size of the subsidy and the definition of "low-income"—would likely affect public opinion regarding a concrete proposal.

We were interested in knowing who was most likely to support funding such as vouchers, so we analyzed the survey responses using multivariate regression. The same explanatory variables used in the other chapters are included here—income, age, education, race, ethnicity, and gender—as well as partisanship and voting in the 2000 election. Controlling for other factors, the individuals most likely to support vouchers to provide computers and Internet access are the young, Democrats, Latinos, African Americans, and the poor. These results are not surprising. Except for younger respondents, those most likely to support government programs to provide computers and Internet access are the least likely to have access to this new technology. Such groups therefore express interest in computers and the Internet as a policy issue. They are also groups that traditionally support a more active role for government in tackling social issues. Vouchers enjoy the support of a little over half the population, with disadvantaged groups most likely to favor subsidies. Yet we foresee some potential problems with vouchers as public policy, as well as benefits, and we recommend a cautious approach.

Our recommendation. We propose a limited experiment with what we call an "educational technology subsidy," or a voucher that is linked to the condition that the recipient is enrolled in some type of further education. Our data lead us to take the position that home access is desirable because of its flexibility and convenience. Our survey shows that interest in many activities, particularly distance learning, decreases when use in a public place is specified. Home Internet and e-mail access are associated with greater levels of digital experience and may play an enabling role for skills development, economic opportunity, and political participation. Home access is associated with more intensive use (and presumably more familiarity with the technology). Ample opportunities for exploration and practice are needed.

For these reasons, we favor experimentation with voucher programs. We hesitate to support handing out vouchers, however, without some provisions for skills development. Our research indicates that issues such as information literacy and even basic literacy limit the use of information technology. Connecting the voucher to educational advancement would also emphasize the public goods potential of information technology, addressing the educational issues that surfaced in both the economic opportunity divide and the democratic divide.

We are in favor of small-scale experimentation only, to test the effectiveness of a voucher program. Despite its limitations, public access may still benefit a larger number of individuals, foster more skills development, and couple technology assistance with information about jobs, education, public services, and community events. The market is also more likely to provide some cheaper solutions for access at home than to solve problems of skills development and literacy. Concern for the latter leads to our final recommendation.

3. *Equal educational opportunity and public investment in lifelong learning.* Our data explored four dimensions of the information technology divide rather than education, but educational issues cropped up at every turn. The ability to use information technology, and to learn and adapt in a changing world, rests upon a general educational foundation. Basic literacy and the ability to locate and evaluate information are academic skills. Education cut across all four divides as the most significant factor other than age, and it is clearly implicated in disparities in economic opportunity and political participation.

Technology promises to magnify some of these inequalities, but it has not created them. As Jennifer Light has argued, Americans have a tendency to seek technological fixes for complex social problems.[21] There are certainly technological aspects at stake, but it is disingenuous to reduce disparities across the four divides to simple questions of access or a few hours of computer training. The underlying problems are two-fold.

First, the quality of American education varies greatly, and poor communities are disadvantaged not only in a relative way, but also, perhaps absolutely, in terms of their ability to prepare students for economic survival and democratic citizenship. Proposals for reforming urban education are rampant, ranging from the equalization of school funding, broad community involvement, business involvement, organizational restructuring, greater accountability through mayoral control, school empowerment, magnet schools, charter schools, vouchers, and proficiency testing. Urban schools have been the focus of a larger educational debate about the quality of public schools, and other low-income communities face some of the same challenges as urban school systems. We hesitate to step into this quagmire of debate and to recommend any specific proposal for improving education, particularly because our research did not directly involve educational issues. Nevertheless, we cannot ignore the fact that our four divides are manifestations of a larger problem of educational opportunity. Society will not truly close any of these gaps without addressing educational inequities.

Second, adults now and in the future will need the ability to secure further education, either to compensate for inadequate preparation in the past or to keep pace with evolving requirements. Rapid technological change, shifts in the labor market, rising skills demands, and instability in employment have made lifelong learning an issue in the economic sphere. Education has always been important for democratic participation, as Thomas Jefferson declared. But the involvement of government in complex and technical issues today far outstrips anything Jefferson could have imagined. Informed participation has become more demanding, because of the growth of initiatives and referenda in the political process, the decline of partisanship, candidate-centered politics, and the proliferation of new sources of political information through the Internet. Lifelong learning may have some advantages in the political sphere as well, if it imparts general skills such as literacy, the ability to analyze and evaluate information, and critical thinking.

Lifelong learning, of course, is a catchall phrase. Depending upon an individual's needs, it may embrace anything from remedial reading classes at a community center to doctoral study. Postsecondary institutions have experienced a surge of nontraditional students returning to the classroom over the past few decades, so trends toward lifelong learning are well underway already. For individuals with limited financial means, however, access to continuing education may be difficult, particularly for vocational or postsecondary training, where tuition is a consideration. American employers offer relatively little job training in comparison with their European counterparts, placing more of the burden on individual workers. Tuition costs have been escalating, as many states seek to balance their beleaguered budgets by cutting subsidies for higher education. Public investment, at all levels of government, can increase the quality and the availability of lifelong learning by supporting adult education and postsecondary institutions. Issues of affordability can be addressed in many ways—for example, through scholarships, loans, grants, tax credits, current funding for job training programs, and government subsidies that hold down general tuition costs. Different solutions are likely needed for different types of continuing education. By investing in lifelong learning, however, we increase the capacity of society to respond to continued change in technology, the economy, and political needs.

The comprehensive high school was an American innovation that responded to the needs of industrialization and urbanization by making education beyond the "3 Rs" available on a widespread basis during the twentieth century.[22] The task for the twenty-first century may well be to insure that all have access to that basic foundation, even on a "second-chance" basis, and that a large number can choose further education according to their interests and qualifications, whether it is specialized vocational training, continuing studies, or postsecondary degrees.

The role of technology should not be viewed in isolation from other challenges to full participation in society. As computers, databases, and the Internet have transformed processes of production and the dissemination of information, they have replicated—and, in some cases, exacerbated—long-standing inequalities. Computers and Internet access will not remedy problems of racism, segregation, unequal education, unequal political participation, and economic inequality, but they represent one dimension of the problem of providing equal opportunity in a democratic society. Public policy that promotes access, skills, and the empowering potential of technology should represent one dimension of the solution as well.

Notes

1. Ordinary least squares multivariate regression is used with the digital literacy index as the dependent variable. The independent variables are income, education, age, gender, ethnicity, race, employment status, home

computer ownership, e-mail address, and home Internet access. See table A6.1.

2. Trotter 2001.

3. National Conference of State Legislatures 2001.

4. See description of Department of Defense budget at the Office of Management and Budget website [www.whitehouse.gov/omb/budget/fy2003/budget/html].

5. Carvin, Conte, and Gilbert 2001, 223; Puma, Chaplin, and Pape 2000. For the distribution of E-Rate dollars, economic need is measured by the percentage of students served by the school or library who participate in the federal school lunch program. For more information about the E-Rate and an initial program evaluation, see especially Puma, Chaplin, and Pape 2000.

6. U.S. Department of Education 2002.

7. Holsendolph 2002; Phillips 2002.

8. Trotter 2001.

9. Trotter 2001.

10. Education Week on the Web 2001.

11. Jesdanun 2002, B1, 4.

12. Hess and Leal 2001.

13. Bushweller 2001; Manzo 2001.

14. Both reference "Moore's Law," developed by Gordon Moore, one of the founders of Intel. Moore predicted that the power of microprocessors would double roughly every eighteen months, creating more powerful computers at a lower cost. Moore's predictions so far have been largely correct. See Thierer 2000 and Compaine 2001, 320.

15. Compaine 2001, xv.

16. Ibid., 115–16.

17. Penuel and Kim 2000.

18. Lacey 2000.

19. Thierer 2000.

20. Both variables are coded as dummy variables, where 1 indicates support for vouchers and 0 otherwise. Because the dependent variables are binary, logistic regression is used. See table A6.2.

21. Light 2001.

22. Goldin 2001.

Appendix I

Multivariate Regression Tables

Table A2.2
Respondent Has Internet Access

Variable	1996 β (se)	1996 p > |z|	1998 β (se)	1998 p > |z|	2000 β (se)	2000 p > |z|
Political factors:						
Strong Democrat	.21 (.19)	.24	.09 (.21)	.68	−.42 (.18)	.02
Strong Republican	−.16 (.21)	.45	.58 (.24)	.02	−.01 (.22)	.95
Pure Independent	.01 (.25)	.96	.02 (.24)	.95	−.46 (.22)	.03
Social factors:						
Log age	−1.0 (.18)	.00	−1.95 (.20)	.00	−2.06 (.20)	.00
Female	.14 (.13)	.30	−.29 (.14)	.04	.11 (.15)	.45
Latino	.08 (.23)	.74	−.35 (.24)	.13	−.29 (.27)	.27
African American	−.04 (.22)	.87	−.64 (.24)	.01	−.97 (.22)	.00
Asian American	.32 (.56)	.57	−.33 (.61)	.58	.10 (.62)	.87
Education	.02 (.04)	.58	.52 (.05)	.00	.54 (.05)	.00
Square income	.01 (.00)	.00	.01 (.00)	.00	−.01 (.00)	.08
Poor	−.15 (.05)	.00	−.14 (.04)	.00	.25 (.06)	.00
Constant	2.07 (.77)	.01	4.66 (.73)	.00	5.31 (.76)	.00
Pseudo-R^2	.1159		.2631		.2536	
Log-reduced χ^2 (11)	184.59	.00	431.45	.00	451.38	.00
N	1,380		1,203		1,346	

Source: American National Election Survey, postelection study, 1996, 1998, and 2000.

Notes: Unstandardized logistic regression coefficients are given. Standard errors are in parentheses. Reported probabilities are based on two-tailed test. Statistically significant coefficients at a confidence interval greater than 90 percent are in bold. For 1996, African Americans constituted 11.9 percent of those surveyed, Asian Americans 1.4 percent, and Latinos 8.7 percent. For 1998, African Americans constituted 11.9 percent, Asian Americans 1.2 percent, and Latinos 10.7 percent. For 2000, African Americans constituted 11.6 percent, Asian Americans 1.8 percent, and Latinos 7.6 percent.

Table A2.3
The Access Divide: Respondent Has Access
to Information Technology

Variable	Internet Access at Home		E-Mail Address		Home Computer	
	β (se)	p .> |z|	β (se)	p >|z|	β (se)	p >|z|
Poor	−.97 (.13)	.00	−.89 (.14)	.00	−1.07 (.13)	.00
Education	.36 (.05)	.00	.55 (.06)	.00	.37 (.05)	.00
Age	−.02 (.00)	.00	−.03 (.00)	.00	−.02 (.00)	.00
Male	.19 (.12)	.12	.26 (.13)	.04	.06 (.13)	.61
Democrat	−.13 (.16)	.00	−.01 (.17)	.94	−.15 (.16)	.35
Republican	.27 (.17)	.12	.30 (.18)	.09	.37 (.18)	.03
Latino	−.52 (.22)	.01	−.75 (.23)	.00	−.79 (.22)	.00
African American	−.69 (.17)	.00	−.66 (.17)	.00	−.40 (.17)	.01
Asian American			.06 (.82)	.93	.32 (.82)	.68
Constant	.82 (.29)	.00	.68 (.30)	.02	1.02 (.30)	.00
N	1,309		1,311		1,319	
Log-reduced χ² (12)	277.16	.00	351.63	.00	275.6	.00
Pseudo R²	.1539		.1981		.1570	

Source: Tolbert, Stansbury, and Mossberger 2001; $N = 1,837$.

Notes: Unstandardized logistic regression coefficients. Standard errors are in parentheses. Probabilities are based on two-tailed test. Statistically significant coefficients at a confidence interval greater than 90 percent are in bold. Survey questions were as follows: "Do you personally have a home computer?" "Do you have an e-mail address with which you can send or receive e-mail?" "Do you have access to the Internet from home?" Responses were coded 1 for agree and 0 for disagree.

Table A3.1
Technical Competence and Information Literacy

Variable	Need More Information Literacy		Need More Technical Competence	
	β (se)	$p > \lvert z \rvert$	β (se)	$P > \lvert z \rvert$
Latino	**.49 (.20)**	**.01**	**.39 (.18)**	**.03**
African American	**.71 (.14)**	**.00**	**.50 (.13)**	**.00**
Asian American	.43 (.54)	.42	.54 (.48)	.26
Poor	**.57 (.12)**	**.00**	**.55 (.11)**	**.00**
Education	**−.51 (.05)**	**.00**	**−.53 (.05)**	**.00**
Male	−.38 (.12)	.11	**−.17 (.10)**	**.00**
Age	**.05 (.00)**	**.00**	**.05 (.00)**	**.00**
Frequency library patronage	**−.23 (.06)**	**.00**	**−.18 (.06)**	**.00**
N	1,545		1,379	
Log-reduced χ^2 (10)	**547.92**	**.00**	**499.13**	**.00**
Pseudo-R^2	.1390		.1521	

Source: Tolbert, Stansbury, and Mossberger 2001; $N = 1,837$.

Notes: Unstandardized ordered logistic regression coefficients. Standard errors in parentheses. Probabilities are based on two-tailed test. Statistically significant coefficients at more then a 90 percent confidence interval in bold. To assess computer literacy, we created an index of responses to the following three questions: Do you need computer assistance (1) locating information on the web, (2) doing homework, or (3) findings books in a library? Variable range is 0–3. To assess the need of respondents for additional technological competence, we created an index of responses to the following three questions: Do you need computer assistance (1) using a mouse or typing, (2) using e-mail, or (3) using word processing or spreadsheet programs. Variable range is 0–3.

Table A3.2
Computer Skills

Variable	Need Computer Skills	
β (se)	*p* >|z|	
Poor	.55 (.11)	.00
Education	-.53 (.05)	.00
Age	.05 (.00)	.00
Male	−.38 (.11)	.00
Latino	.31 (.18)	.08
African American	.52 (.13)	.00
Asian American	−.02 (.48)	.97
Frequency library patronage	−.02 (.06)	.00
N	1,311	
Log-reduced χ^2 (10)	545.93	.00
Pseudo R^2	.1112	

Source: Tolbert, Stansbury, and Mossberger 2001; *N* = 1,837.

Notes: Unstandardized ordered logistic regression coefficients. Standard errors in parentheses. Probabilities are based on two-tailed test. Statistically significant coefficients at a confidence interval greater than 90 percent are in bold. This table was used to generate the probabilities reported in chapter 3. To assess the need of respondents for computer skills, we created an index of responses to the following six questions: Do you need computer assistance (1) using a mouse and typing, (2) using e-mail, (3) locating information on the web, (4) using word processing/spreadsheet programs, (5) doing homework, or (6) finding books in a library? Variable range is 0–6.

Table A3.3
Attitudes about Library Use

Variable	Consider the Library a Community Meeting Place		Support Public Access for Computers and Internet	
	β (se)	p >|z|	β (se)	p >|z|
Poor	.29 (.12)	.01	−.21 (.11)	.04
Education	.01 (.05)	.81	.10 (.04)	.03
Age	.00 (.00)	.15	−.00 (.00)	.69
Male	−.21 (.11)	.05	−.09 (.10)	.35
Latino	.55 (.19)	.00	−.26 (.17)	.12
African American	.48 (.14)	.00	.65 (.13)	.00
Asian American	−.25 (.44)	.56	−1.12 (.36)	.00
Frequency library patronage	.22 (.06)	.00		
N	1,549		1,399	
Log-reduced χ^2 (10)	56.09	.00	53.52	.00
Pseudo-R^2	.0261		.0111	

Source: Tolbert, Stansbury, and Mossberger 2001; N = 1,837.

Notes: Model 1 unstandardized logistic regression coefficients, standard errors in parentheses; probabilities are based on two-tailed test. Model 2 unstandardized ordered logistic coefficients, standard errors in parentheses; probabilities are based on two-tailed test. Statistically significant coefficients at a confidence interval greater than 90 percent are in bold. To assess respondents' support for public access to computers and the Internet, we created an index of responses to six questions. Would you use a computer or access the Internet at a (1) recreation center, (2) senior center, (3) local church, (4) government office, (5) public library, or (6) public school after hours? Variable range is 0–6.

Table A3.4
Instructional Preferences

Variable	Opposed to One-on-One Instruction		Opposed to Group Instruction		Opposed to Online Instruction		Opposed to Printed Manuals	
	β (se)	p >|z|	β (se)	p >|z|	β (se)	p >|z|	β (se)	p >|z|
Poor	.17	.13	.15	.16	**.19**	**.08**	−.04	.73
	(.11)		(.11)		**(.11)**		(.11)	
Education	**−.08**	**.07**	**−.09**	**.05**	**−.12**	**.01**	.05	.30
	(.05)		**(.05)**		**(.05)**		(.05)	
Age	**.01**	**.04**	**.01**	**.00**	**.01**	**.00**	**.01**	**.03**
	(.00)		**(.00)**		**(.00)**		**(.00)**	
Male	**.24**	**.02**	.15	.15	**−.27**	**.01**	−.11	.26
	(.10)		(.10)		**(.10)**		(.10)	
Latino	.04	.80	**−.30**	**.09**	−.02	.93	−.01	.97
	(.18)		**(.18)**		(.17)		(.17)	
African American	.09	.49	**−.44**	**.00**	**−.39**	**.00**	**−.31**	**.02**
	(.13)		**(.13)**		**(.13)**		**(.13)**	
Asian American	.12	.76	**.87**	**.03**	.30	.44	−.62	.13
	(.40)		**(.40)**		(.39)		(.40)	
Frequency library patronage	**−.10**	**.07**	−.06	.28	**−.00**	**.95**	.01	.84
	(.06)		(.06)		**(.05)**		(.05)	
N	1,563		1,561		1,545		1,558	
Log-reduced χ^2 (10)	**24.78**	**.00**	**43.47**	**.00**	**45.80**	**.00**	**17.37**	**.03**
Pseudo-R^2	.0074		.0118		.0113		.0044	

Source: Tolbert, Stansbury, and Mossberger 2001; *N* = 1,837.

Notes: Unstandardized ordered logistic regression coefficients, standard errors in parentheses; probabilities are based on two-tailed test. Statistically significant coefficients at a confidence interval greater than 90 percent are in bold. Dependent variables were measured on a five-point ordinal scale: 1 = strongly agree, 2 = agree, 3 = neutral, 4 = disagree, and 5 = strongly disagree.

Table A4.1
Attitudes about Computers and Economic Opportunity

Variable	Believe Using Computer Necessary to Keep Up with the Times		Need to Learn New Computer Skills for Career Advancement	
	β (se)	p >|z|	β (se)	p >|z|
Poor	−.03 (.13)	.80	.02 (.11)	.86
Education	.05 (.05)	.33	−.02 (.04)	.73
Age	−.01 (.00)	.22	**−.01 (.00)**	**.01**
Male	−.11 (.12)	.33	**−.20 (.10)**	**.04**
Latino	**.75 (.23)**	**.00**	.15 (.17)	.36
African American	**.63 (.16)**	**.00**	**.50 (.13)**	**.00**
Asian American	.84 (.56)	.13	.44 (.41)	.29
Unemployed	.24 (.15)	.11	**.38 (.12)**	**.00**
Constant	**.69 (.26)**	**.00**		
N	1,512		1,543	
Log-reduced χ^2 (8)	**32.93**	**.00**	**38.77**	**.00**
Pseudo-R^2		.02	.01	—

Source: Tolbert, Stansbury, and Mossberger 2001; $N = 1,837$.

Notes: Coefficients reported in model 1 are unstandardized logistic regression estimates; standard errors are in parentheses. Coefficients reported in model 2 are unstandardized ordered logistic regression estimates; standard errors are in parentheses. Statistically significant coefficients at a confidence interval greater than 90 percent are in bold. Constant is not estimated in ordered logit models. Probabilities are based on two-tailed test. We measured responses to the following questions: These days, do you think it is necessary for people to use the Internet to keep up with the times? (agree coded 1, and disagree coded 0) and Do you believe you need to learn new computer skills to get a job? Do you believe you need to learn computer skills to get a higher paying job? Do you believe you need to learn computer skills to get a promotion? Do you believe you need to learn new computer skills to start a small business? Variable range is 0–4.

Table A4.2
Support Use of Internet for Employment and Education

Variable	Would Search for a Job Online		Would Take a Class Online	
	β (se)	p >|z|	β (se)	p >|z|
Latino	−.06 (.23)	.78	**−.32 (.20)**	**.00**
African American	**.30 (.17)**	**.07**	.24 (.16)	.12
Asian American	.30 (.66)	.64	**−1.30 (.44)**	**.00**
Poor	−.04 (.14)	.78	**−.49 (.13)**	**.00**
Education	**.31 (.06)**	**.00**	**.24 (.06)**	**.00**
Male	**.39 (.13)**	**.00**	−.03 (.12)	.80
Age	**−.04 (.00)**	**.00**	**−.02 (.00)**	**.00**
Unemployed	**−.30 (.15)**	**.05**	**−.33 (.15)**	**.02**
Constant	**1.63 (.28)**	**.00**	**1.07 (.27)**	**.00**
N	1,434		1,412	
Log-reduced χ² (8)	**220.60**	**.00**	112.56	**.00**
Pseudo-R²		.13	.06	—

Source: Tolbert, Stansbury, and Mossberger 2001; *N* = 1,837.

Notes: Unstandardized logistic regression coefficients; standard errors are in parentheses; probabilities are based on two-tailed test. Statistically significant coefficients at a confidence interval greater than 90 percent are in bold. We measured responses to the following questions: How do you feel about searching or applying for a job online? How do you feel about taking a class online? Positive responses were coded 1, and negative responses were coded 0.

Table A4.3
Support Use of Internet for Employment and Education in a Public Place

Variable	Would Search for a Job Online in a Public Place		Would Take a Class Online in a Public Place	
	β (se)	$p >\lvert z \rvert$	β (se)	$p >\lvert z \rvert$
Latino	.16 (.21)	.45	−.05 (.19)	.79
African American	**.66 (.16)**	**.00**	**.33 (.14)**	**.02**
Asian American	−.33 (.48)	.48	−.60 (.44)	.17
Poor	−.06 (.13)	.64	−.05 (.12)	.65
Education	**.15 (.05)**	**.00**	−.02 (.04)	.56
Male	**.45 (.12)**	**.00**	**.26 (.11)**	**.02**
Age	**−.03 (.00)**	**.00**	**−.00 (.00)**	**.00**
Unemployed	−.02 (.14)	.88	−.08 (.13)	.51
Constant	**1.36 (.26)**	**.00**	**.55 (.24)**	**.02**
N	1,417		1,418	
Log-reduced χ^2 (8)	**140.85**	**.00**	25.97	**.00**
Pseudo-R^2		.07	.01	—

Source: Tolbert, Stansbury, and Mossberger 2001; N = 1,837.

Notes: Unstandardized logistic regression coefficients; standard errors in parentheses; probabilities are based on two-tailed test. Statistically significant coefficients at a confidence interval greater than 90 percent are in bold. We measured responses to the following questions: How do you feel about searching or applying for a job online in a public place? How do you feel about taking a class online in a public place? Positive responses were coded 1, and negative responses were coded 0.

Table A4.4
Respondents' Internet Use for Employment and Education

Variable	Searched for a Job Online		Taken a Class Online	
	β (se)	p >|z|	β (se)	p >|z|
Latino	−.03 (.22)	.89	.19 (.30)	.51
African American	**.53 (.16)**	**.00**	**.96 (.20)**	**.00**
Asian American	.57 (.50)	.25	.85 (.51)	.10
Poor	.03 (.15)	.85	−.31 (.20)	.12
Education	**.44 (.06)**	**.00**	**.20 (.08)**	**.01**
Male	**.40 (.13)**	**.00**	.26 (.17)	.12
Age	**−.06 (.01)**	**.00**	**−.02 (.00)**	**.00**
Unemployed	**−.42 (.13)**	**.02**	**−.66 (.26)**	**.00**
Constant	.27 (.29)	.35	**−1.86 (.40)**	**.00**
N	1,523		1,525	
Log-reduced χ^2 (8)	**369.98**	**.00**	**81.01**	**.00**
Pseudo-R^2		.1965	.07	—

Source: Tolbert, Stansbury, and Mossberger 2001; N = 1,837.

Notes: Unstandardized logistic regression coefficients; standard errors are in parentheses; probabilities are based on two-tailed test. Statistically significant coefficients at a confidence interval greater than 90 percent are in bold. We measured responses to the following questions: Have you searched or applied for a job online? Have you taken a class online? Agree was coded 1, and disagree was coded 0.

Table A5.1
Support for Digital Democracy and E-Government

Variable	Voting		Voter Registration		Looking Up Government Information		Town Meetings	
	β (se)	p >|z|	β (se)	p >|z|	β (se)	p >|z|	β (se)	p >|z|
Poor	−.11 (.14)	.40	−.10 (.11)	.48	**−.32 (.17)**	**.05**	**−.30 (.14)**	**.03**
Education	**.33 (.05)**	**.00**	**.40 (.05)**	**.00**	**.42 (.07)**	**.00**	**.22 (.05)**	**.00**
Age	**−.02 (.00)**	**.00**	**−.03 (.00)**	**.00**	**−.02 (.00)**	**.00**	**−.01 (.00)**	**.00**
Male	.14 (.12)	.25	**.28 (.13)**	**.03**	.16 (.16)	.29	**.26 (.12)**	**.04**
Democrat	**.46 (.16)**	**.00**	**.34 (.16)**	**.04**	**.41 (.20)**	**.03**	.10 (.16)	.51
Republican	.06 (.17)	.69	.07 (.17)	.67	.27 (.21)	.19	.07 (.17)	.65
Latino	−.10 (.23)	.66	−.27 (.23)	.24	**−.53 (.26)**	**.04**	.11 (.23)	.61
African American	−.25 (.17)	.14	−.22 (.17)	.20	−.10 (.21)	.61	.01 (.17)	.93
Asian American	−.18 (.67)	.78	−.37 (.72)	.60	**−1.17 (.72)**	**.10**	−.51 (.66)	.43
Voter	**.32 (.16)**	**.04**	**.38 (.16)**	**.02**	**.62 (.19)**	**.00**	**.52 (.16)**	**.00**
Constant	−.41 (.30)	.16	.29 (.30)	.33	**.73 (.36)**	**.04**	−.40 (.30)	.19
N	1,167		1,227		1,210		1,118	
Log-reduced χ^2 (12)	107.15	.00	162.15	.00	111.17	.00	73.39	.00
Pseudo-R^2	.0663		.0995		.0935		.0474	

Source: Tolbert, Stansbury, and Mossberger 2001; *N* = 1,837.

Notes: Unstandardized logistic regression coefficients; standard errors are in parentheses; probabilities are based on two-tailed test. Statistically significant coefficients at a confidence interval greater than 90 percent are in bold. We measured responses to the following questions: How do you feel about voting in a government election online? How do you feel about registering to vote online? How do you feel about looking up government information online? and How do you feel about participating in an online town meeting? Positive responses were coded 1, and negative responses were coded 0.

Table A5.2
Support for Digital Democracy vs. Actual Experience

Variable	Support for Online Participation		Support for Online Participation in Public Place		Experience with Online Political Participation	
	β (se)	p >|z|	β (se)	p >|z|	β (se)	p >|z|
Poor	**−.22 (.13)**	**.09**	**−.36 (.12)**	**.00**	**−.28 (.12)**	**.02**
Education	**.37 (.05)**	**.00**	**.17 (.05)**	**.00**	**.40 (.05)**	**.00**
Age	**−.02 (.00)**	**.00**	**−.01 (.00)**	**.00**	**−.03 (.00)**	**.00**
Male	**.27 (.12)**	**.02**	**.20 (.11)**	**.07**	**.43 (.11)**	**.00**
Democrat	**.35 (.15)**	**.02**	.35 (.14)	.15	.09 (.14)	.50
Republican	.08 (.16)	.59	**.28 (.15)**	**.06**	−.11 (.15)	.45
Latino	−.30 (.22)	.17	.07 (.20)	.72	−.06 (.20)	.75
African American	−.14 (.16)	.36	.04 (.15)	.78	−.15 (.15)	.33
Asian American	−.52 (.55)	.34	−.71 (.54)	.19	−.79 (.56)	.15
Participate	**.48 (.15)**	**.00**	**.36 (.14)**	**.01**	**.60 (.14)**	**.00**
N	963		1,185		1,251	
Log-reduced χ² (10)	151.65	.00	77.13	.00	230.04	.00
Pseudo-R²	.0505		.0262		.0741	

Source: Tolbert, Stansbury, and Mossberger 2001; N = 1,837.

Notes: Unstandardized ordered logistic regression coefficients; standard errors are in parentheses; probabilities are based on two-tailed test. Statistically significant coefficients at a confidence interval greater than 90 percent are in bold. To measure support for online political participation, we created an index of responses to the following four questions: How do you feel about (1) voting in a government election online, (2) registering to vote online, (3) looking up government information online, and (4) participating in an online town meeting? Variable range is 0–4. To measure support for public online political participation, we created an index of responses to the following three questions: How do you feel about (1) voting in a government election online in a public place, (2) registering to vote online in a public place, and (3) looking up government information online in a public place? Variable range is 0–3. To measure experience with online political participation, we created an index of responses to the following three questions: Have you (1) searched for political information online, (2) looked up information on government services online, and (3) seen an online political advertisement? Variable range is 0–3.

Table A6.1
Digital Experience

Variable	Digital Experience	
	β (se)	$p > |z|$
Poor	−.00 (.09)	.99
Education	**.34 (.03)**	**.00**
Age	**−.04 (.00)**	**.00**
Male	**.40 (.08)**	**.00**
Home Computer	.14 (.13)	.29
E–mail address	**1.38 (.12)**	**.00**
Home Internet Access	**.47 (.14)**	**.00**
Latino	.02 (.14)	.84
African American	.15 (.10)	.13
Asian American	−.27 (.32)	.40
Unemployed	**−.26 (.10)**	**.01**
Constant	**2.30 (.19)**	**.00**
N	1,454	
F	**124.006**	**.00**
Adjusted R^2	.482	

Notes: Unstandardized OLS regression coefficients; standard errors are in parentheses; probabilities are based on two-tailed test. This variable measures experience using computers and the Internet for various transactions and is an index of responses to seven questions. Has the respondent (1) located information on the web, (2) searched for political information online, (3) looked up information on government service online, (4) applied for or searched for a job online, (5) taken a class online, (6) used the computer to do homework, or (7) used the computer to find books in the library without assistance? Variable range is 0–7.

Table A6.2
Support for Vouchers

Variable	Support Vouchers to Low-Income Persons for Computers		Support Vouchers to Low-Income Persons for Internet Access	
	β (se)	p >|z|	β (se)	p >|z|
Poor	**.39 (.16)**	**.01**	**.31 (.15)**	**.04**
Education	−.09 (.06)	.16	−.01 (.06)	.83
Age	**−.01 (.00)**	**.00**	**−.00 (.00)**	**.07**
Male	−.16 (.14)	.23	.09 (.13)	.46
Democrat	**.56 (.18)**	**.00**	**.57 (.17)**	**.00**
Republican	**−.64 (.18)**	**.00**	**−.58 (.17)**	**.00**
Latino	**.79 (.28)**	**.01**	**.84 (.27)**	**.00**
African American	**.93 (.23)**	**.00**	**.56 (.19)**	**.00**
Asian American	.22 (.86)	.79	1.26 (1.11)	.25
Participate	−.10 (.18)	.56	−.21 (.17)	.21
Constant	**1.53 (.34)**	**.00**	**.61 (.31)**	**.05**
N	1,075		1,095	
Log–reduced χ^2 (10)	**161.38**	**.00**	**121.07**	**.00**
Pseudo-R^2	.1181		.0833	

Source: Tolbert, Stansbury, and Mossberger 2001; $N = 1,837$.

Notes: Unstandardized logistic regression coefficients; standard errors are in parentheses; probabilities are based on two-tailed test. Statistically significant coefficients at a confidence interval greater than 90 percent are in bold. To measure support for a voucher system to assist low-income persons to purchase computers, we created an index based on responses to the question, How do you feel about a government program to provide computers for the low income? To measure support for a voucher system to assist low-income persons gain access to the Internet, we created an index based on responses to the question, How do you feel about a government program to fund Internet access for low income or rural residents? For both measures, positive responses are coded 1, and negative responses are coded 0.

Appendix 2

Survey Questionnaire

Question FIRST

[DIAL TELEPHONE NUMBER AND PRESS ANY KEY TO CONTINUE]

[USE FI THROUGHOUT THE SURVEY TO MAKE NOTES CONCERNING THE INTERVIEW]

[PAR] Hi, this is [NAME] from Kent State. We started an interview about computers and Internet use. We would really appreciate it if you could finish the interview now. Do you have time? [PRESS ANY KEY OR QUIT]

[REF] Hello, this is [NAME], a student calling from the Department of Sociology at Kent State University. Earlier this (wk/mo) you or someone in your household declined to be interviewed in a survey concerning computer and Internet use. We really would like your opinion for our study. Do you have time to answer a few questions? [PRESS ANY KEY OR QUIT]

Question INTRODUCTION

Hi, my name is [INTERVIEWER NAME] and I'm a student at Kent State University in Kent, Ohio. I'm helping researchers at Kent State investigate issues about computers and Internet use. The interview only takes about 8 minutes. Will you help us?

1. CONTINUE
2. REFUSAL

3. CALLBACK
4. BUSINESS
5. COMMUNICATION BARRIERS
6. PHONE ISSUES
7. NO ADULT AT HOME
8. ALREADY INTERVIEWED

Question PHONE

Enter the correct phone disposition

1. NO ANSWER
2. BUSY
3. ANSWERING MACHINE (IS DEFINITELY A HOUSEHOLD)
4. ANSWERING MACHINE (UNSURE WHETHER IT IS A HOUSE-HOLD OR BUSINESS)
5. FAX/DATA LINE
6. PAGER/CELL PHONE
7. DISCONNECTED/NONWORKING NUMBER
8. NUMBER CHANGED
9. PRIVACY MANAGER
10. CALL FORWARDING
11. TECHNICAL PHONE ISSUES

Question COMMBARR

Enter the correct communication disposition

1. LANGUAGE (CANNOT UNDERSTAND PERSON ON PHONE)
2. PHYSICALLY OR MENTALLY UNABLE/INCOMPETENT
3. MISCELLANEOUS

Question CALLBACK

Is there a better day or time I could call back?

1. QUALIFIED RESPONDENT NOT IDENTIFIED
2. QUALIFIED RESPONDENT IDENTIFIED

Question REFUSAL

1. HANG-UP AT THE INTRODUCTION SCREEN
2. REFUSAL AT THE INTRODUCTION SCREEN
**USED PERSUADERS/QUALIFIED RESPONDENT NOT IDENTIFIED

Question CONSENT

Drs. Tolbert, Stansbury, and Mossberger at Kent State University are conducting a study about computers and Internet use. This interview is completely voluntary, and you may terminate the interview at any time. All information that you share with us is strictly anonymous. This means that there will be no way to associate you with the information you give. Also, if you do not want to answer any particular question just tell me and I'll skip to the next one. This study has been approved by Kent State University. If you have further questions that you would like addressed before you participate in the study, you may call Dr. Tolbert at 330-672-2060, or they can call you back at your convenience.

[PRESS ANY KEY TO CONTINUE]

Question SCREEN

Are you 21 years or older?

1. Yes
2. No
3. Don't know/not applicable

Question QUALIFICATION

Can I speak to someone in the household who is 21 years or older?

1. Yes
2. No
3. Don't know/not applicable

Question Q1

Do you personally have a home computer?

1. Yes
2. No
3. Don't know/not applicable

Question Q2

In the last month, how often did you personally use a computer at . . .

work
home
school
a library or community center
a friend's or relative's house
. . . for any reason.

[READ THROUGH ANSWER CHOICES]

1. 0 times
2. 1–10 times
3. 11–30 times
4. 31–100 times
5. More than 100 times

Question Q3

Do you have an e-mail address through which you can send or receive e-mail by computer?

1. Yes
2. No
3. Don't know/not applicable

Question Q4

In the last month, how often did you access the Internet from . . .
work
home
school
a library or community center
a friend's or relative's house
. . . for any reason.

[READ THROUGH ANSWER CHOICES]

1. 0 times
2. 1–10 times
3. 11–30 times
4. 31–100 times
5. More than 100 times

Question Q5

How do you access the Internet or an online service from home?

1. Web TV
2. Telephone line and modem
3. DSL
4. Broadband or cable modem
5. None
6. Don't know/not applicable

Question Q6

These days, do you think it is necessary for people to use the Internet if they want to keep up with the times?

[YES—NECESSARY; NO—NOT NECESSARY]

1. Yes
2. No
3. Don't know/not applicable

Question Q7

Have you ever been turned down for a job because you needed to know more about computers?

1. Yes
2. No
3. Don't know/not applicable

Question Q8

Have your computer skills ever helped you get a job or a promotion?

[YES—HELPED; NO—HAVEN'T HELPED]

1. Yes
2. No
3. Don't know/not applicable

Question Q9

Do you believe you need to learn new computer skills to get a . . . (Name all that apply)

1. Job
2. Promotion
3. Higher-paying job
4. Start a small business
5. None
6. Don't know/not applicable

Question Q10

I am going to read you a list of activities people can do online. For each activity, please tell me if you have used the Internet in this way?

Searched for political information
Looked for information on government services or contact a government official

Seen a political campaign ad
Searched or applied for a job
Taken a class

[YES—USED INTERNET; NO—DID NOT USE INTERNET]

1. Yes
2. No
3. Don't know/not applicable

Question Q11

How do you feel about the following statements?
(Answer agree, neutral, or disagree)

I would . . .

vote in a government election online
register to vote online
look up government information online
search or apply for a job online
take a class online
participate in an online town meeting

1. Agree
2. Neutral
3. Disagree
4. Don't know/don't care/other

Question Q12

Would you use a computer located in a public place to . . . ?
(Read the following response categories)

1. Vote in an election
2. Register to vote
3. Look up information about government services
4. Search or apply for a job
5. Take a class online
6. Don't know/not applicable

Question Q13

I am going to read you a list of possible places to use computers and access the Internet. For each location, please tell me if you would be willing to go there?
(Read the following response categories)

Recreation center
Senior center
Local church
Government office
Library
Public schools after hours
Don't know/not applicable/other

Question Q14

Please tell me if you would need assistance doing the following computer task:

Using the mouse and typing
Using e-mail
Locating information on the Internet
Using word processing/spreadsheet programs
Taking a class online
Doing homework
Finding books

1. Yes
2. No
3. Don't know/not applicable

Question Q15

If you need to learn a new computer or Internet skill, how would you prefer to be taught that skill?

Personal instruction
Take a class
Use online help or tutorials
Use printed manuals
(Answer agree, neutral, or disagree)

1. Agree
2. Neutral
3. Disagree
4. Don't know/don't care/other

Question Q16

In the last month, how frequently have you visited a library for any
reason?

1. 0 times
2. 1–5 times
3. 6–10 times
4. 11–15 times
5. More than 15 times
6. Don't know/not applicable

Question Q17

Do you think of the library as a community gathering place?

1. Yes
2. No
3. Don't know/not applicable

Question Q18

There should be a government program to partially fund the cost of
a home computer for low-income individuals.
 (Answer agree, neutral, or disagree)

1. Agree
2. Neutral

3. Disagree
4. Don't know/don't care/other

Question Q19

There should be a government program to partially fund the cost of
Internet access for low-income individuals or those living in rural
areas.
(Answer agree, neutral, or disagree)

1. Agree
2. Neutral
3. Disagree
4. Don't know/don't care/other

Question Q20

Some people are registered to vote and others are not. Are you registered to vote in the precinct or election district in which you now live?

1. Yes
2. No
3. Don't know/not applicable

Question Q21

Did you vote in the 2000 presidential elections?

1. Yes
2. No
3. Don't know/not applicable

Question Q22

Generally speaking, do you usually consider yourself a . . .

1. Republican
2. Democrat

3. Independent
4. Don't know/not applicable/other

Question Q23

How would you describe your views on most political matters? Generally do you think of yourself as . . .

1. Liberal
2. Moderate
3. Conservative
4. Don't know/not applicable/other

Question Q24

How many people live in your household?
1. Actual number of people
2. Refused

Question Q25

What was the last grade in school you completed?
1. Not a high school graduate
2. High school graduate
3. Some college
4. College graduate
5. Postgraduate work or degree (Master's, M.B.A., J.D., M.D., and Ph.D.)
6. Don't know/not applicable

Question Q26

How old are you?
1. Actual age between 18 and 98
2. Refused

Question Q27

Are you . . .
1. White or caucasian
2. Black or African American
3. Asian
4. Other (specify)
5. Refused

Question Q28

Are you of Latino origin or descent?
1. Yes
2. No
3. Don't know/not applicable

Question Q29

Was your total family income in 2000 OVER $30,000?
1. Under
2. Over
3. Refused

Question Q30 [income]

Would you say . . .
$25,000–$30,000
$20,000–$25,000
$15,000–$20,000
$10,000–$15,000
$5,000–$10,000
Under $5,000
Refused
Don't know/not applicable

Question Q31

At this time do you receive any form of public assistance, such as food stamps, section 8 housing vouchers, TANF, Medicaid, SSI disability?

1. Yes
2. No
3. Don't know/not applicable

Question Q32 [income]

Would you say . . .
$30,000–$50,000
$50,000– $75,000
$75,000–$100,000
$100,000–$125,000
Over $125,000
Refused
Don't know/not applicable

Question Q33

What is your current employment status?

1. Currently employed
2. Temporarily out of work
3. Not in the market for work
4. Full-time student
5. Retired
6. Don't know/not applicable

Question Q34

This concludes the interview. Thank you for your time.
[DO NOT ASK THIS QUESTION. DETERMINE GENDER]

1. Male
2. Female
3. Don't know/not applicable

Question THANK

Thank you for your time.

[PRESS ANY KEY TO CONTINUE]

Glossary

ANES   American National Election Survey

CATI   Computer-Assisted Telephone Interviewing laboratory at Kent State University that conducted the telephone survey used in this study

CPS   Current Population Survey, U.S. Census Bureau

CTC   Community technology center, a federal program to assist communities with technology needs, such as hardware, software, content development, and training

digital divide   Disparities in information technology based on demographic factors such as race, ethnicity, income, education, and gender

distance learning   Education or training delivered through use of the Internet or other technology, such as the television

DSL   form of high-speed Internet access called a "digital subscriber line"

e-commerce   Commercial business transactions, such as purchases, conducted over the Internet

e-democracy   Civic engagement using e-mail, online discussion lists or chat rooms, and websites for political mobilization and participation

e-government   The delivery of information and services online via the Internet or other digital means

E-Rate program   Established through the Telecommunications Act of 1996, it offers considerable discounts on telecommunications technologies to libraries and schools (ranging from 20 percent to 90 percent). The depth of the discount is calculated on the basis of economic need, with some additional priority given to rural locations. Funded by taxes on local and long distance telephone carriers, provides schools and libraries in poor communities with discounted rates for Internet access, high-speed data connections, phone service, and wiring

GED   General education development credential

NALS   National Adult Literacy Survey

NTIA   National Telecommunications and Information Administration

PC   Personal computer

SCANS   Secretary's Commission on Achieving Necessary Skills

TOP   Technologies Opportunities Program is a federal program to assist communities with technology needs, such as hardware, software, content development, and training

References

Abramson, P. R. 1983. *Political attitudes in America.* San Francisco: Freeman.

ActionForum. 2000. Berkeley general plan ActionForum. Available [online]: www.actionforum.com/forum/index.html?forum_id=10 [30 March 2003].

Alvarez. R. M., and J. Nagler. 2002. The likely consequences of Internet voting for political representation. *Loyola of Los Angeles Law Review* 34 (3): 1115–53.

American Association of School Librarians (with the Association for Educational Communications and Technology). 1998. *Information power: Building partnerships for student learning.* Chicago: American Library Association.

American Library Association. 1989. *Presidential committee on information literacy.* Available [online]: www.infolit.org/documents/89Report.htm [23 May 2002].

American National Election Survey. 1996. Available [online]: www.icpsr. umich.edu [10 January 2002].

———. 1998. Available [online]: www.icpsr.umich.edu [10 January 2002].

———. 2000. Available [online]: www.icpsr.umich.edu [10 January 2002].

Appelbaum, E., and P. Albin. 1998. Computer rationalization and the transformation of work: Lessons from the insurance industry. In *The changing nature of work,* edited by F. Ackerman, N. R. Goodwin, L. Dougherty, and K. Gallagher, 153–56. Washington, D.C.: Island Press.

Association of College and Research Libraries. 2000. *Information literacy competency standards for higher education.* Available [online]: www.ala.org/acrl/ ilcomstan.html [30 March 2002].

Atkinson, R. D., and R. H. Court. 1998. *The new economy index: Understanding America's economic transformation and new economy project.* Available [online]: www.neweconomyindex.org [8 March 2002].

Baldassare, M. 2000. *California in the new millennium: The changing social and political landscape.* Berkeley: University of California Press.

Barber, B. 1984. *Strong democracy.* Berkeley: University of California Press.

Barrington, L. 2000. *Does a rising tide lift all boats? America's full-time working poor reap limited gains in the new economy.* Conference Board Report 1271–00-RR. Washington, D.C.: Conference Board.

Benner, J. 2002. Bush plan "digital distortion." *Wired News* (February 7). Available [online]: *www.wired.com/news/print/0,1294,50279,00.html* [15 May 2002].

Benton Foundation. 1996. *Buildings, books, and bytes: Libraries and communities in the digital age, a report on the public's opinion of library leaders' visions for the future.* Washington, D.C.: Benton Foundation.

Bernhardt, A., M. Morris, M. S. Handcock, and M. A. Scott. 2001. *Divergent paths: Economic mobility in the new American labor market.* New York: Russell Sage Foundation.

Bimber, B. 1999. The Internet and citizen communication with government: Does the medium matter? *Political Communication* 16 (4): 409–28.

———. 2001. Information and political engagement in America: The search for effects of information technology at the individual level. *Political Research Quarterly* 54 (1): 53–67.

Bowler, S., and T. Donovan. 1998. *Demanding choices.* Ann Arbor: University of Michigan Press.

Bowler, S., T. Donovan, and C. Tolbert, eds. 1998. *Citizens as legislators: Direct democracy in the United States.* Columbus: Ohio State University Press.

Brookings Institution. 2002. *The future of Internet voting.* A symposium cosponsored by the Brookings Institution and Systems, Inc., January 20. Available [online]: www.brookings.org/comm/transcripts/20000120.htm [15 May 2002].

Bucy, E. P. 2000. Social access to the Internet. *Harvard International Journal of the Press-Politics* 5 (1): 50–61.

Budge, I. 1996. *The new challenge of direct democracy.* Cambridge, Mass.: Blackwell.

Bushweller, Kevin. 2001. Beyond machines. *Education Week on the Web.* Available [online]: www.edweek.org/sreports/tc01/tco/article.cfm?slug=35pittsburgh.h20 [10 July 2002].

Butler, D., and Ranney, A. 1994. *Referendums around the world: The growing use of direct democracy.* Washington, D.C.: AEI Press.

Campbell, A., P. E. Converse, W. E. Miller, and D. E. Stokes. 1960. *The American voter.* Chicago: University of Chicago Press.

Cancian, M., and D. R. Meyer. 2000. Work after welfare: Women's work effort, occupation, and economic well being. *Social Work Research* 24 (2): 69–86.

Carnevale, A. P., and S. J. Rose. 2001. Low earners: Who are they? Do they have a way out? In *Low-wage workers in the new economy,* edited by R. Kazis and M. C. Miller, 45–66. Washington, D.C.: Urban Institute Press.

Carvin, A., with C. Conte and A. Gilbert. 2001. The E-rate in America: A tale of four cities. In *The digital divide: Facing a crisis or creating a myth?* edited by B. M. Compaine, 223–42. Cambridge, Mass.: MIT Press.

Castells, M. 2000. *The rise of the network society.* 2d ed. Oxford: Blackwell.

Chadwick, A., with Christopher May. 2001. Interaction between states and citizens in the age of the Internet: E-government in the United States, Britain, and the European Union. Presented at the annual meeting of the American Political Science Association, 30 August–2 September, San Francisco.

Chew, F. 1994. The relationship of information needs to issue relevance and media use. *Journalism Quarterly* 71: 676–88.

Chow, C., J. Ellis, J. Mark, and B. Wise. 1998. *Impact of CTCNet affiliates: Findings from a national survey of users of community technology centers.* Available [online]: www.ctcnet.org/impact98.htm [25 March 2003].

Civille, R. 1995. The Internet and the poor. In *Public access to the Internet,* edited by B. Kahin and J. Keller, 175–207. Cambridge, Mass.: MIT Press.

Clarke, S. E., and G. L. Gaile. 1998. *The work of cities.* Minneapolis: University of Minnesota Press.

Clift, S. 2000. The e-democracy e-book: Democracy is online 2.0. Available [online]: www.e-democracy.org.do [12 January 2002].

Compaine, B. M., ed. 2001. *The digital divide: Facing a crisis or myth?* Cambridge, Mass.: MIT Press.

Conway, M. 1991. *Political participation in the United States.* 2d ed. Washington, D.C.: CQ Press.

Davis, R. 1999. *The web of politics: The Internet's impact on the American political system.* New York: Oxford University Press.

Davis, R., and D. Owen. 1998. *New media and American politics.* New York: Oxford University Press.

Dionne, E. J. 1996. *They only look dead: Why progressives will dominate the new political era.* New York: Simon & Schuster.

Dryzek, J. S. 1990. *Discursive democracy: Politics, policy and political science.* Cambridge: Cambridge University Press.

Dutton, W. H. 1999. *Society on the line: Information politics in the digital age.* Oxford: Oxford University Press.

Education Week on the Web. 2001. *The new divides, technology counts 2001.* Available [online]: www.edweek.org/sreports/tc01article.cfm?slug=35execsum.h20 [10 July 2002].

Ellwood, D. T. 2000. Winners and losers in America: Taking the measure of the new economic realities. In *A working nation: Workers, work, and government in the new economy,* edited by D. T. Ellwood, R. M. Blank,

J. Blasi, D. Kruse, W. A. Niskanen, and K. Lynn-Dyson, 1–41. New York: Russell Sage Foundation.

Evelyn, J. 2002. Nontraditional students dominate undergraduate enrollments, U. S. study finds. *Chronicle of Higher Education.* Available [online]: http://chronicle.com/free/2002/2002060402n.htm [10 June 2002].

Fagan, J. C., and B. D. Fagan. 2001. Citizens' access to on-line state legislative documents. *Government Information Quarterly* 14 (2): 173–89.

Fishkin, J. 1993. *Democracy and deliberation.* New Haven, Conn.: Yale University Press.

Fountain, J. E. 2001. *Building the virtual state: Information technology and institutional change.* Washington, D.C.: Brookings Institution.

Gartner Group. 2000. Key issues in e-government strategy and management. *Research notes, key issues.* Stanford, Calif.: Gartner Group.

Gerber, E. R. 1999. *The populist paradox.* Princeton, N.J.: Princeton University Press.

Gibson, R. 2002. Elections online: Assessing internet voting in light of the Arizona Democratic Primary. *Political Science Quarterly* (winter): 561–83.

Ginsburg, L., J. Sabatini, and D. A. Wagner. 2000. Basic skills in adult education and the digital divide. In *Learning to bridge the digital divide,* 77–89. Paris: Organization for Economic Cooperation and Development.

Gladden, T., and C. Taber. 2000. Wage progression among less skilled workers. In *Finding jobs: Work and welfare reform,* edited by D. Card and R. M. Blank, 160–92. New York: Russell Sage Foundation.

Goldin, C. 2001. *The human capital century and American leadership: Virtues of the past.* National Bureau of Economic Research working paper 8239. Available [online]: www.nber.org/papers/w8239 [10 May 2002].

Greengard, S. 1998. Going for the distance: As the technology advances, more and more employees are reaping the benefits of distance learning. *Industry Week* 247 (9): 22–23.

Grossman, L. 1995. *The electronic commonwealth.* New York: Penguin.

Hague, B., and B. Loader. 1999. *Digital democracy: Discourse and decision-making in the information age.* London: Routledge.

Hall, D. T., and P. Mirvis. 1995. Careers as lifelong learning. In *The changing nature of work,* edited by A. Howard, 323–64. San Francisco: Jossey-Bass.

Hart-Teeter. 2000. E-government: The next American revolution. Prepared for the Council for Excellence in Government. Available [online]: www.excelgov.org [5 December 2001].

Heldrich (John J.) Center for Workforce Development. 2002. One-stop innovations: Leading change under the WIA one-stop system. Prepared for the U.S. Department of Labor/Employment and Training Administration/Office of Workforce Security. Available [online]: www. heldrich.rutgers.edu/Resources/Publication/85/ PromisingPracticesFullReport.pdf [25 May 2002].

Herzenberg, S., J. Alic, and H. Wial. 1998. *New rules for a new economy: Employment and opportunity in postindustrial America.* Ithaca, N.Y.: Cornell University Press.

Hess, F. M., and D. L. Leal. 2001. A shrinking digital divide? The provision of classroom computers across urban school systems. *Social Science Quarterly* 82 (4): 765–78.

Ho, A. T. 2002. Reinventing local governments and the e-government initiative. *Public Administration Review* 62 (4): 434–44.

Hochschild, J. L. 1995. *Facing up to the American dream: Race, class, and the soul of the nation.* Princeton, N.J.: Princeton University Press.

Hochschild, J. L., and N. Scovronick. 2000. Democratic education and the American Dream. In *Rediscovering the democratic purposes of education,* edited by L. M. McDonnell, P. M. Timpane, and R. Benjamin, 209–42. Lawrence: University Press of Kansas.

Hoffman, D. L., T. P. Novak, and A. Schlosser. 2000. The evolution of the digital divide: How gaps in internet access may impact electronic commerce. *Journal of Computer Mediated Communication* 5 (3). Available [online]: www.ascusc.org/jcmc/vol5/issue3/hoffman.html [15 February 2001].

Hoffman, D. L., T. P. Novak, and A. E. Schlosser. 2001. The evolution of the digital divide: Examining the relationship of race to Internet access and usage over time. In *The digital divide: Facing a crisis or creating a myth?* edited by B. M. Compaine, 47–98. Cambridge, Mass.: MIT Press.

Holsendolph, E. 2002. U.S. sees future, and it is broadband. *Atlanta Journal and Constitution,* 29 September, 6P.

Holzer, H. J. 1996. *What employers want: Job prospects for less-educated workers.* New York: Russell Sage Foundation.

Horrigan, J. B., and L. Rainie. 2002. Getting serious online (Pew Internet and American Life Project). Available [online]: www.pewinternet.org/ reports/pdfs/ PIP_Getting_Serious_Online3ng.pdf [10 March 2002].

Initiative and Referenda Institute. 2002. Ballotwatch. Available [online: www.iandrinstitute.org [8 June 2002].

International Technology Education Association. 2002. Executive summary of standards for technological literacy. In *Standards for technological literacy: Content for the study of technology,* 2d ed. Available [online]: www.iteawww.org/TAA/STLexesum.htm [20 March 2003].

James, E. 2001. Learning to bridge the digital divide. *OECD Observer* 224: 43–45.

Jefferson, T. [1816] 1988. A letter to Samuel Kercheval. In *Political thought in America: An anthology*, edited by M. B. Levy, 160–62. Chicago: Dorsey Press.

Jesdanun, A. 2002. Battle over digital divide moves to homefront: Internet use up, but minorities and poor less likely to have home hookup. *Akron Beacon-Journal*, 18 March, B1.

Johnson, J. H., Jr. 2002. A conceptual model for enhancing community competitiveness in the new economy. *Urban Affairs Review* 37 (6): 763–79.

Kaestle, C. F., A. Campbell, J. D. Finn, S. T. Johnson, and L. J. Mickulecky. 2001. *Adult literacy and education in America: Four studies based on the National Adult Literacy Survey.* NCES publication number 2001534. Washington, D.C.: U.S. Department of Education, National Center for Education Statistics. Available [online]: http://nces.ed.gov/pubsearch/pubsinfo.asp?pubid=2001534 [23 May 2002].

Kasarda, J. D. 1990. City jobs and residents on a collision course: The urban underclass dilemma. *Economic Development Quarterly* 4 (4): 286–307.

Kettl, D. 2000. *The global public management revolution: A report on the transformation of governance.* Washington, D.C.: Brookings Institution.

King, G. 1997. *A solution to the ecological inference problem.* Cambridge, Mass: Harvard University Press.

King, G., M. Tomz, and Jason Wittenberg. 2000. Making the most of statistical analysis: Improving interpretation and presentation. *American Journal of Political Science* 44: 347–361.

Kirsch, I. S., A. Jungeblut, L. Jenkins, and A. Kolstad. 2002. *Adult literacy in America: A first look at the findings of the National Adult Literacy Survey.* 3d ed. NCES publication number 1993-275. Washington, D.C.: U.S. Department of Education, National Center for Education Statistics. Available [online]: nces.ed.gov/pubs93/93275.pdf [20 March 2003].

Kruse, D., and J. Blasi. 2000. The new employer-employee relationship. In *A working nation: Workers, work, and government in the new economy,* edited by D. T. Ellwood, R. M. Blank, J. Blasi, D. Kruse, W. A. Niskanen, and K. Lynn-Dyson, 42–91. New York: Russell Sage Foundation.

Lacey, M. 2000. Clinton to seek U.S. subsidies to help the poor get online. *New York Times*, 22 January, A7.

Layne, K., and J. W. Lee. 2001. Developing fully functional e-government: A four-stage model. *Government Information Quarterly* 18 (2): 122–36.

Lewis, M. M. 2001. *Next: The future just happened.* New York: W. W. Norton.

Light, J. S. 2001. Rethinking the digital divide. *Harvard Educational Review* 71 (4): 709–33.

Magleby, D. 1984. *Direct legislation: Voting on ballot propositions in the United States.* Baltimore: Johns Hopkins University Press.

Mann, H. [1839] 1988. The necessity of education in a republican government. In *Political thought in America: An anthology*, edited by M. B. Levy, 209–16. Chicago: Dorsey Press.

Manzo, K. K. 2001. Academic record. *Education Week on the Web.* Available [online]: www.edweek.org/sreports/tc01/tc01article.cfm?slug=35academic.h20 [10 July 2002].

Margolis, M., and D. Resnick. 2000. *Politics as usual: The cyberspace "revolution."* Thousand Oaks, Calif.: Sage.

Markle Foundation. 1999. Government programs involving citizen access to Internet services. Available [online]: http://fdncenter.org/pnd/19990727/webreview.html [2 August 2002].

McChesney, R. 1999. *Rich media, poor democracy: Communication policy in dubious times.* Urbana: University of Illinois Press.

McGuckin, R. H., and B. Van Ark. 2001. *Making the most of the information age: Productivity and structural reform in the new economy.* Perspectives on a Global Economy. Conference Board report 1301–07-RR. Washington, D.C.: Conference Board.

McMahon, C., and C. Bruce. 2002. Information literacy needs of local staff in cross-cultural development projects. *Journal of International Development* 14: 113–27.

McNeal, R., C. Tolbert, K. Mossberger, and L. Dotterweich. 2003. "Innovating in digital government in the American states." *Social Science Quarterly* 84 (1). In press.

Melitski, J. 2001. The world of e-government and e-governance. Available [online]: *www.aspanet.org* [5 January 2002].

Mendolsohn, M., and A. Parkin, eds. 2001. *Referendum democracy: Citizens, elites, and deliberation in referendum campaigns.* New York: MacMillan.

Mickelson, R. A. 1996. Opportunity and danger: Understanding the business contribution to public education. In *Implementing educational reform: Sociological perspectives on educational policy*, edited by K. M. Borman, P. W. Cookson, Jr., A. R. Sadounk, and J. Z. Spade, 245–72. Norwood, N.J.: Ablex.

Mishel, L., J. Bernstein, and J. Schmitt. 2001. *The state of working America: 2000–2001.* Ithaca, N.Y.: Cornell University Press/ILR Press.

Moss, P., and C. Tilly. 2001. *Stories employers tell: Race, skill, and hiring in America.* New York: Russell Sage Foundation.

Mossberger, K. 2000. *The politics of ideas and the spread of enterprise zones.* Washington, D.C.: Georgetown University Press.

National Academy of Sciences. 1996. Summary and recommendations. In *Measuring poverty: A new approach.* Available [online]: www.nap. edu/readingroom/books/poverty/summary.html [8 September 2002].

National Center for Education Statistics (NCES). (n.d.). Defining and measuring literacy. Available [online]: http://nces.ed.gov/naal/defining/defining.asp [23 May 2002].

National Conference of State Legislatures. 2001. Information technology and Internet laws. Available [online]: www.ncsl.org/programs/lis/legislation/ITlaws01.htm [15 July 2002].

National Performance Review. 1993. From red tape to results: Creating a government that works better and costs less. Washington, D.C.: Government Printing Office.

Neu, C. R., R. H. Anderson, and T. K. Bikson. 1999. *Sending your government a message: E-mail communication between citizens and government.* Santa Monica, Calif.: RAND.

Nie, N., and L. Erbring. 2000. *Internet and society: A preliminary report.* Stanford, Calif.: Stanford Institute for the Quantative Study of Society, Stanford University. Available [online]: www.stanford.edu/group.siqss/press_release/preliminary_report.pdf [10 February 2002].

Niskanen, W. A. 2000. Creating good jobs and good wages. In *A working nation: Workers, work, and government in the new economy,* edited by D. T. Ellwood, R. M. Blank, J. Blasi, D. Kruse, W. A. Niskanen, and K. Lynn-Dyson, 92–104. New York: Russell Sage Foundation.

Norris, D. F., P. D. Fletcher, and S. Holden. 2001. Is your local government plugged in? Highlights of the 2000 Electronic Government Survey. Prepared for the International City/County Management Association and Public Technology, Inc. Available [online]: www.umbc.edu/mipar/final_draft/PDFs/e-gov.icma.final-4-25-01.pdf [10 June 2002].

Norris, P. 1999. *Critical citizens: Global support for democratic governance.* Oxford: Oxford University Press.

———. 2001. *Digital divide: Civic engagement, information poverty, and the Internet worldwide.* New York: Cambridge University Press.

Novak, T. P., D. L. Hoffman, and A. Venkatesh. 1997. Diversity on the Internet: The relationship of race to access and usage. Presented at the Aspen Institute Forum on Diversity and the Media, October 1997.

Office of Management and Budget. 2002. United States budget fiscal year 2003. Available [online]: www.whitehouse.gov/omb/budget/fy2003/budget.html [10 July 2002].

Organization for Economic Cooperation and Development. 2000. *Learning to bridge the digital divide.* Paris: Organization for Economic Cooperation and Development.

Osborne, D., and T. Gaebler. 1992. *Reinventing government: How the entrepreneurial spirit is transforming the public sector.* Reading, Mass. Addison-Wesley.

Osterman, P. 1999. *Securing prosperity: The American labor market: How it has changed and what to do about it.* Princeton, N.J.: Princeton University Press.

————. 2001. Employers in the low-wage/low-skill labor market. In *Low-wage workers in the new economy*, edited by R. Kazis and M. S. Miller, 67–87. Washington, D.C.: Urban Institute Press.

Pateman, C. 1970. *Participation and democratic theory.* New York: Cambridge University Press.

Pear, R. 2002. Number of people living in poverty increases in U.S. *New York Times*, 25 September, A1.

Pearson, G., and T. A. Young, eds. 2002. *Technically speaking: Why all Americans need to know more about technology.* Washington, D.C.: National Academy of Engineering Committee on Technological Literacy.

Penuel, W., and D. Kim. 2000. Promising practices and organizational challenges in community technology centers. Available [online]: www.sri.com/policy/ctl/assets/images/vStreets_Promising_Practices.pdf.

Peters, B. G. 1996. *The Future of governing: Four emerging models.* Lawrence: University Press of Kansas.

Pew Internet and American Life Project. 2000. African-Americans and the Internet by T. Spooner and L. Rainie. Available [online]: www.pewinternet.org/reports/pdfs/PIP_African_Americans_Report.pdf [5 January 2002].

————. 2002. The rise of the e-citizen: How people use government agencies' web sites. By E. Larsen and L. Rainie. Pew Internet and American Life Project. Available [online]: www.pewinternet.org/reports/pdfs/PIP_Govt_Website_Rpt.pdf [15 August 2002].

Pew Research Center. 2000. Campaign and Internet survey. October 10–November 25. Available [online]: www.pewinternet.org/datasets/index.asp [5 January 2002].

Phillips, H. F. 2002. Making a case for net access. *San Jose Mercury News*, 1 October, 3C.

Piven, F. F., and R. A. Cloward. 1988. *Why Americans don't vote.* New York: Pantheon.

Puma, M. J., D. D. Chaplin, and A. D. Pape. 2000. *E-rate and the digital divide: A preliminary analysis from the integrated studies of educational technology.* Washington, D.C.: Urban Institute. Available [online]: www.urban.org/education/erate.html [10 July 2002].

Putnam, R. 2000. *Bowling alone: The collapse and revival of American community.* New York: Simon & Schuster.

Rangarajan, A., P. Schochet, and D. Chu. 1998. *Employment experiences of welfare recipients who find jobs: Is targeting possible?* Princeton, N.J.: Mathematica Policy Research, Inc. Available [online]: www.mathinc. com [10 January 2002].

Rheingold, H. 1993. *The virtual community: Homesteading on the electronic frontier.* Reading, Mass.: Addison-Wesley.

Rosenstone, S. J., and M. Hansen. 1993. *Mobilization, participation, and democracy in America.* New York: Macmillan.

Rosenthal, A. 1997. *The decline of representative democracy.* Washington, D.C.: CQ Press.

Salamon, L. M. 1991. Overview: Why human capital? Why now? In *An economic strategy for the 90s: Human capital and America's future*, edited by D. W. Hornbeck and L. M. Salamon, 1–39. Baltimore: Johns Hopkins University Press.

Saulny, S. 2001. New jobless centers offer more than a benefit check. *New York Times*, 5 September, A1, A21.

Schattschneider, E. E. 1960. *The semi-sovereign people.* New York: Holt, Rinehart, and Winston.

Scheufele, D., and D. Shah. 2000. Personality strength and social capital: The role of dispositional and informational variables in the production of civic participation. *Communication Research* 27 (2): 107–31.

Secretary's Commission on Achieving Necessary Skills. 1992. Learning a living: A blueprint for high performance: a SCANS report for America 2000. Available [online]: http://wdr.doleta.gov/SCANS/lal/lal.htm [5 January 2002].

Seifert, J. and E. Petersen. 2002. The promise of all things E? Expectations and challenges of emergent electronic government. *Perspectives on Global Development and Technology* 1 (2): 193–212.

Servon, L. J., and M. K. Nelson. 2001. Community technology centers: Narrowing the digital divide in low-income, urban communities. *Journal of Urban Affairs* 23: 279–90.

Shadid, A. 2001. Report shows narrowing digital divide: GAO finds net use up in rural areas, among minorities. *Boston Globe,* 22 February, C1.

Shah, D., N. Kwak, and R. Holbert. 2001. "Connecting" and "disconnecting" with civic life: Patterns of Internet use and the production of social capital. *Political Communication* 18: 141–62.

Sipple, J. W., C. G. Miskel, T. M. Matheney, and C. P. Kearney. 1997. The creation and development of an interest group: Life at the intersection of big business and education reform. *Educational Administration Quarterly* 33: 440–73.

Smith, E. 1989. *The unchanging American voter.* Berkeley: University of California Press.

Solop, F. I. 2000. Digital democracy comes of age in Arizona: Participation and politics in the first binding Internet election. Presented at Annual Meeting of the American Political Science Association, 31 August–3 September, Washington, D.C.

Stiglitz, J. E., P. R. Orszag, and J. M. Orszag. 2000. The role of government in a digital age. Commissioned by the Computer and Communications Industry Association. Available [online]: www.ccianet.org/ digital_age/report.pdf [20 August 2002].

Stone, D. 2002. *Policy paradox: The art of political decision making.* Rev. ed. New York: Norton.

Stowers, G. N. L. 1999. Becoming cyberactive: State and local governments on the World Wide Web. *Government Information Quarterly* 16 (2): 111–27.

Strawn, J., and K. Martinson. 2001. Promoting access to better jobs: Lessons for job advancement from welfare reform. In *Low-wage workers in the new economy,* edited by R. Kazis and M. S. Miller, 111–34. Washington, D.C.: Urban Institute Press.

Sunstein, C. 2001. Freedom of expression in the United States: The future. In *The boundaries of freedom of expression and order in American democracy,* edited by T. Hensley, 319–47. Kent, Ohio: Kent State University Press.

Swaim, P. L., R. M. Gibbs, and R. Teixeira. 1998. Introduction to *Rural education and training in the new economy: The myth of the rural skills gap,* edited by R. M. Gibbs, P. L. Swaim, and R. Teixeira, 3–22. Ames: Iowa State University Press.

Tapscott, D. 1997. The digital media and the reinvention of government. *Canadian Public Administration* 40 (2): 328–45.

Teixeira, R., and D. A. McGranahan. 1998. Rural employer demand and worker skills. In *Rural education and training in the new economy: The myth of the rural skills gap,* edited by R. M. Gibbs, P. L. Swaim, and R. Teixeira, 115–30. Ames: Iowa State University Press.

Thierer, A. D. 2000. *How free computers are filling the digital divide.* Report no. 1361. Heritage Foundation Backgrounder. Available [online]: www.heritage.org/library/backgrounder/bg1361.html [5 January 2002].

Thurow, L. C. 1999. *Building wealth: The new rules for individuals, companies, and nations in a knowledge-based economy.* New York: Harper-Collins.

Toffler, A. 1995. *Creating a new civilization: The politics of the third wave.* Kansas City, Mo.: Turner.

Tolbert, C., and R. McNeal. 2003. Does the Internet increase voter turnout in elections? *Political Research Quarterly* 56:2.

Tolbert, C., M. Stansbury, and K. Mossberger. 2001. Defining the digital divide: Survey. Available from authors [ctolber1@kent.edu].

Trotter, A. 2001. Closing the digital divide. *Education Week on the Web.* Available [online]: www.edweek.org/sreports/tc01article.cfm?slug=35 solutions.h20 [10 July 2002].

Uchitelle, L. 1999. Devising new math to define poverty: Millions more would be poor in fresher census formula. *New York Times,* 18 October, A1, A14.

U.S. Census Bureau. 2000. Quick Tables. QT-PE, Race and Hispanic or Latino: 2000. Data Set: Census 2000 Summary File 1 (SF 1) 100-Percent Data; Geographic Area: Berkeley city, California. Available [online]: http://factfinder.census.gov/bf/_lang=e?_SF1_U_QTP3_ goe_id=16000US0606000.htm [10 June 2002].

————. 2001. Income 2000. Table 1. Available [online]: www.census.gov/hhes/income/income00/inctab1.html [30 March 2003].

————. 2002a. Poverty 2001. Available [online]: www.census.gov/ hhes/poverty/threshld/thresh01.html [30 March 2003].

————. 2002b. Income 2001. Table 1. Available [online]: www. census.gov.hhes/income/income01/inctab1.html [30 March 2003].

U.S. Department of Commerce. 1995. National Telecommunication and Information Administration. *Falling through the net: A survey of the "Have Nots" in rural and urban America.* Available [online]: www. ntia.doc.gov/ntiahome/fallingthru.html [18 March 2002].

————. 1998. National Telecommunication and Information Administration. *Falling through the net II: New data on the digital divide.* Available [online]: www.ntia.doc.gov/ntiahome/net2/falling.html [18 March 2002].

————. 1999. National Telecommunication and Information Administration. *Falling through the net: Defining the digital divide.* Available [online]: www.ntia.doc.gov/ntiahome/fttn99/FTTN.pdf [18 March 2002].

————. 2000a. *Background for digital economy 2000 report.* Available [online]: http://osecnt13.osec.doc.gov/public.nsf/docs/ 5E4B499384543E86852568F5006F1AA4 [2 March 2002].

————. 2000b. National Telecommunications and Information Administration. *Falling through the net: Toward digital inclusion.* Available [online]: www.esa.doc.gov/fttn00.htm [18 March 2002].

————. 2002. National Telecommunication and Information Administration. *A nation online: How Americans are expanding their use of the Internet.* Available [online]:www.ntia.doc.gov/ntiahome/dn/ anationonline2.pdf [18 March 2002].

U.S. Department of Education. 2002. ED programs that help bridge the digital divide. Available [online]: www.ed.gov/Technology/digdiv.html [27 August 2002].

U.S. Department of Labor. 1999. *Futurework: Trends and challenges for work in the 21st century.* Available [online]: www.dol.gov/dol/asp/public/futurework/report/chapter2/main.htm [10 February 2000].

———. 2002. Employment and Training Adminstration. *Workforce investment act; Lower living standard income level.* Available [online]: http://wsdc.doleta.gov/llsil01.asp [July 10, 2002].

Verba, S., K. L. Schlozman, and H. E. Brady. 1995. *Voice and equality: Civic voluntarism in American politics.* Cambridge, Mass.: Harvard University Press.

Verba, S., and N. H. Nie. 1972. *Participation in America.* New York: Harper & Row.

Walsh, E. O, with M. E. Gazala and C. Ham. 2001. The truth about the digital divide. In *The digital divide: Facing a crisis or creating a myth?* edited by B. M. Compaine, 279–84. Cambridge, Mass.: MIT Press.

Weber, L. M., and J. Bergman. 2001. Who participates and how? A comparison of citizens "online" and the mass public. Presented at the Annual Meeting of the Western Political Science Association, 15–17 March, Las Vegas.

West, D. M. 2000. *Assessing e-government: The Internet, democracy, and service delivery by state and federal governments.* Washington, D.C.: World Bank. Available [online]: www1.worldbank.org/publicsector/egov/EgovReportUS00.htm [21 June 2002].

———. 2001. E-government and the transformation of public sector service delivery. Presented at the annual meeting of the American Political Science Association, August 30–September 2, San Francisco.

———. Forthcoming. E-government and the transformation of service delivery and citizen attitudes. *Public Administration Review.*

Wilhelm, A. 2000. *Democracy in the digital age: Challenges to political life in cyberspace.* New York: Routledge.

Wolfinger, R., and S. J. Rosenstone. 1980. *Who votes?* New Haven, Conn.: Yale University Press.

Wright, G. 2002. Groups, lawmakers protest Bush plan to cut programs to bridge digital divide. Gannett News Service (May 26). Available [online]: www.detnews.com/2002/technology/0205/15/technology-489537.htm [10 June 2002].

Index